There's a writer-spea
Cat Got Your Thumb? gently enc
and shows us how. With playful imagery that is
identifiable and entertaining, basic rules of grammar, and hints about how to turn simple observation into electrifying storytelling, this installment of Jay Speyerer's "Legacy legacy" is an enjoyable, helpful, and at times, hilarious read!
Nancy Van Iderstine
Writer, Fox Home Entertainment

Cat Got Your Thumb? reminded me to slow down and pay more attention to the specifics of my life. Jay knows how to capture everyday details with refreshing newness. He's a nuance wizard who makes reading a pleasure.
Hank Walshak
Author, Writer, Presentation Coach

Cat Got Your Thumb? liberates the art of communication from its academic prison. Jay Speyerer writes with a common-sense, humorous style that taps into the potential of our language and how it can enrich our lives.
William Loeffler
Playwright, Features/ Pittsburgh Tribune-Review

Jay's recipe for communication:
Place incident in (metaphorical) bowl
Add heaping dollops of humor
Blend vigorously to create unexpected twists and turns
Allow to ferment
Read communication story with eager eyes
Serves everyone!
Patty Kreamer
Speaker, Author of …But I Might Need It Someday!

Yes! It is important to remember the tastes and smells of Christmas long years ago. And what a wonderful exercise to explore the pockets of that old jacket in the closet with your mind's eye! Jay gives us helpful and fun tips for getting started in the writing process.
Margaret Randall
Founder, TellOurLifeStories.com

Also by Jay Speyerer

The Stories of Our Days
The Story System

Cat Got Your Thumb?

Cat Got Your Thumb?

Communicating across distance, cultures, generations, and even species

by

Jay Speyerer, TLD, SFA*

Legacy Road Communications
Pittsburgh, Pennsylvania

*These Letters Don't Stand For Anything

ISBN-10: 0-9764729-9-6
ISBN-13: 978-0-9764729-9-5

Published by: Legacy Road Communications, LLC
www.legacyroad.net

This book was printed in the United States of America.

Contents

These articles fall into more than one category, hence the tricky table of contents. It's divided into sections, each of which holds a story that might fit just as snugly into another category.

Writing

Communication in General

Non verbal

Speaking

Memoir Writing

to the creatures

two-legged and four,
in feathers, fabric, or fur,
who inform the contents of this book

Recognition

My thanks and appreciation go out to:

Joanne Sujansky and Hank Walshak for cogent comments on the content.

Anita Buzzy Prentiss for getting the best out of Lulu and me in the cover photograph. (Lulu's roommate, Fleck, refused to participate, citing weight issues.) All of the other photos are by yours truly.

Donna Herrle of Drawing Conclusions for transforming the photo into the vibrant cover design.

And my friend Patty Kreamer for the title of the signature story and, ultimately, this book.

Introduction

Over the course of the last couple of years, these articles have appeared in my on-line publication, the *Legacy Road Communiqué*, and in other publications, both paper and pixel. Now you have them all in one volume.

In this collection of observations on the oddities of human communication, you will find:

cats
dogs
turkeys
deer
ducks
chipmunks
and a butterfly.

Because this book is about *human* communication, you'll also find many humans, all engaged in such affirming activities as teaching, getting married, traveling, observing, and generally interacting with each other. The animals provide metaphors for communication. The people provide examples of it, good and not so.

Because I'm an educator at heart, you'll also find entertaining information on such things as body language, e-mail, eye contact, voice control, cultural confusion, story telling, and our way of using the English language, both written and spoken, good and not so.

You will also find shameless cultural references (Mark Twain, Daniel Webster, and Winston Churchill) and ditto, pop cultural references (John Stamos, O.J. Simpson, and Richard Gere). And we'll visit a couple of nice restaurants in Los Angeles, both of them good.

I repeat... the book is about communication. I never said it wasn't wide-ranging.

Jay

1

Cat Got Your Thumb?

OPEN YOUR *FAUX PAS* FILES

I was holding this cat, see, and trying to protect it from a dog. For my trouble, I got my thumb bitten … by the cat. All because of one dumb move on my part.

Dumb, but useful.

My friend Maureen has two cats and a big, galumphing Redbone Coonhound named Quigley, who adores me. Quigley couldn't love me more if I were a combination of Lassie, the Dog Whisperer, and the inventor of Gravy Train. But he and the cats don't get along, and that's why he spends most of his time on the first floor of the house, and the cats live on the second.

I was visiting one Friday evening, and after I had played with Quigley, I went upstairs to say hi to one of the cats, Stitch. The dog stood watch at the bottom of the steps. In retrospect, it probably wasn't the smartest move I ever made to let Quigley see me holding Stitch.

My memory of the ensuing events is fractured because of how quickly they happened, but in a nutshell...
Quigley races up the steps, Maureen behind him.
I hold Stitch away from him.
The dog grabs the cat's leg. (No damage.)
Maureen grabs the dog.
Stitch bites my thumb to get away. (It works. And there's plenty of damage.)

Four puncture wounds and a ragged tear later, I'm bleeding in the sink of the upstairs bathroom, cleaning the ball of my thumb with soap and water and Bactine™ (that stuff really stings, so it must work) and applying pressure with gauze and band-aids. Maureen is concerned, wondering aloud about the emergency room, a tetanus shot, and stitches. I nix the ideas; I'd had a shot in recent memory, and I want nothing more to do with anything called stitch.

The point of this story? Pick one. Even though the upshot of the event is that I made a bonehead move, it's still a story, and as such, has applicable value. In no special order of importance, here are a few possible topics for illustration:

1. Cats are ingrates.
2. Dogs are jealous.
3. When cats panic, they chomp down on the nearest available piece of meat.
4. It's a perfect illustration of irony. The very beast I'm trying to save from pain inflicts it on me.

5. It illustrates an old saying, one that had always mystified me: no good deed goes unpunished.
6. Humans cannot reason with animal instinct.
7. The human body's power to heal itself is a source of amazement.
8. We can wonder at the suddenness of random events.
9. Seemingly innocent actions can have dire consequences. (All I wanted to do was pet the damn cat.)
10. Did I mention that cats are ingrates?

I can use this lapse in judgment to illustrate these and other points in my presentations and articles. That's true of your goofs, too. Whereas most people would love to bury such mental lapses and never be reminded of them again, that doesn't apply to writers and speakers. For normal people, such events are embarrassments. For us, they're material.

I don't know when or if I'll use this story, but it's there if I need it. So take the plunge and air out your own lapses. You'd be surprised at how much mileage you can get out of one story. And if you show that you're human and that you make mistakes, your audience will like you more.

By the way, my friend Stitch is fine. Quigley and I are still pals, but to Stitch, he's *canis non grata.* And my thumb has healed nicely, but if you're looking for a hand model, I'm not your guy.

2

Put a Spring in Your Voice

FIVE TECHNIQUES TO KEEP YOUR VOICE LIVELY

Everyone with a normal vocal apparatus has voice control. You need this control if you speak publicly, including business meetings and presentations, seminars, conducting a class... any venue where you must be persuasive. And you can do this, because everyone has some degree of control. We can all put a spring in our voice.

This control comes in five overlapping areas:

Pitch Volume Tone Stress Inflection

Pitch: Your pitch can always be lower or higher relative to your baseline pitch (your normal speaking voice). We all have range, but the amount varies. Generally, a lower pitch sounds more authoritative. Nervousness, anger, and anxiety can raise the pitch. Try to lower it a bit. Think of the baseline pitch as the first floor of a house. Lowering the pitch doesn't mean going down to the sub-basement. But when we're nervous, we might end up on the 2nd floor or even the roof. For normal conversation, stay on the first floor. For authority, try halfway down the cellar steps.

Volume: The amount of volume you need depends on the space in which you're speaking and, of course, whether you have a microphone. Assuming you don't have a mic, the need will vary with the room and its acoustics. In a confined space with bare floors and few people, you need less volume. In a large space with a lot of people and soft surfaces to absorb your voice, you'll need more. More volume means more breath and more constriction of the vocal folds. Be careful with volume control: there's a tendency to raise pitch along with volume. This could result in a voice with more volume, but with less authority.

Tone: here it means overall tone of voice. Nasal and soft vs. sharp and piercing. Whiny vs. assured. Monotone vs. varied. Monotone is one of the highest on the list of vocal transgressions, and for good reason: it's sleep-inducing. Where do you think the word *monotonous* comes from? Other tones to be aware of include aggressive, tentative, brash, forceful, and sarcastic. You should strive for a tone of authority, without the brash or aggressive qualities. Breathy voices sound shy and less forceful. The higher the pitch and the more breathiness, the less the perceived authority.

Stress means emphasis. Stressed (or "punched") words are sounded differently so they stand out. You can emphasize a word by raising the pitch or lowering it (see "inflection").

By increasing the volume: Come here right **NOW**.

By drawing out consonants: Come here *rrrright nnnnow.* (Aside: Not every consonant can be extended. Don't try it with the plosives like *b* and *p*, or you'll pop a vein.)

By pausing before the word: Come here right ... now.

Even by whispering it: Come here right now.

Inflection: raising or lowering pitch in various parts of sentence. In other words, the direct opposite of monotone. In addition to being a way to punch selected words —

Come here ↗ right ↘
now

— a rising inflection is the way English speakers indicate that the sentence is a question.

Could you come here right ↗ now?

Another transgression you should avoid is so-called "upspeak."

That's when even a statement sounds like a ↗ question(?)

Practice controlling your voice in these five areas. This control allows you to put that spring in your voice and to control your message and, by extension, the reaction of your audience. You're standing at the front of the room, so that means you're in charge. You should also be in charge of your voice.

3

55 - 38 - 7

LIES, DAMNED LIES, AND THE MISUSE OF STATISTICS

Occasionally, you'll hear communication trainers (this writer included) refer to Albert Mehrabian's research on "apportionment of meaning." This term refers to how we receive information from the sender in a one-on-one conversation. The common interpretation is that we receive 55 per cent of the other person's meaning from physical cues (body language and facial expression), 38 per cent from tone of voice, and only seven per cent from the actual spoken words. Some trainers attribute these figures to all spoken communication. They are incorrect.

Mehrabian's work can be easily misinterpreted if his research is not studied carefully. I recently heard a speaker dismiss facile references to this numbers game because (he said) Mehrabian was referring only to messages indicating whether someone was liking or disliking something. The speaker was also incorrect, but at least he was closer.

The 55-38-7 percentages refer to evaluating *inconsistent* messages from the sender, wherein the words say one thing but the face and body say another. And these evaluations are of the *implicit* messages that are conveyed about feelings: pleasure-displeasure, arousal-nonarousal, dominance-submissiveness, and like-dislike. Here Mehrabian is referring only to messages that can be sent implicitly, and these messages are emotional, not factual.

You cannot send an inconsistent message about a fact: "The meeting is at 2:00." You can send an inconsistent message about a feeling or an attitude: "I think this meeting is very interesting and informative." (Said while yawning, rolling your eyes, and looking at your watch.) Here, the spoken message is overwhelmed by the unspoken. In his book, *Silent Messages*, Mehrabian says: "When any implicit behavior contradicts speech, it is more likely to determine the total impact of the message."

And that message is only about emotions or attitudes, not facts.

4

Spellcheck and Other Slavic Heroes

SPELLCHECK ISN'T FULL PROOF

I read something interesting recently, and I forget where, so my acknowledgments and apologies to the writer. The owner of a company says that s/he does not want her/his employees to use the spellcheck feature, because it makes them lazy and dependent. I agree, but the employees of that company must be conscientious beyond the norm. I have found that many document creators know the feature exists, but for all they care about it, Spellcheck might as well be the name of the U.N. ambassador from Belarus.

Many of you reading this are good spellers, or at least you proofread your e-mails and paper documents before you release them into the world. So this article isn't directed at you, but read on anyway. Maybe a friend needs some help.

However, for those of you who write – and I use the word "write" charitably – a document and then send it off without so much as checking to see that you spelled the recipient's name correctly (or even your own), keep reading.

The spellcheck feature is an aid, not a cure. The human element must play the lead role because of a necessary distinction in writing: there's misspelling and there's misuse. Sometimes the two overlap.

Some common and not-so-common examples of misuse:

To, too, two. We know the meanings of theses words and they are not interchangeable. *To* should never be substituted for *too.*

There, their, they're. Same here.

Know, no, now. I've seen all three confused with each other, and the confusion is unnecessary if you think about it. One of the words is even pronounced differently.

Are, our. Speaking of pronunciation, I saw these words swapped for each other often when I was grading college essays. The students would use *are* and *our* interchangeably because of sloppy enunciation; they pronounced *both* words as *are.* As a result, they wrote them the same way. And by now those former students are in our business world, possibly committing the same transgressions. You know who you are.

It's, its. Here is the counterintuitive part of our topic. The exception to the rule, if you will. *Its* is possessive (see below about the dog losing its bone); *it's* is a contraction for *it is.* You learned in school that one job of an apostrophe is to signify possession. True, except where the word *it* is concerned. The other job of an apostrophe is to stand in for missing letters, as in the contraction *don't* (missing *o* in *not*), *they're* (missing *a* in *are*), and of course *it's* (missing *i* in *is*).

Plural and possessive. Nouns become plural when you add *s* or *es*. You do not make a word plural by using an apostrophe. Ever. That includes numbers. Example: The 1960s and 1970s were turbulent decades. The only exceptions to the no-apostrophe-for-plurals rule are for single lower case letters and abbreviations with internal periods, and that's to avoid confusion. Ex: Mind your p's and q's with her because she has two M.A.'s.

The spelling checker can't help you with many of these situations, whether it's the feature installed as part of your word processor or e-mail program, or one of the on-line versions such as spellcheck.net or grammarstation.com. (Spellcheck.net knows spelling but not usage, so I'm not including its results in the following examples.) Grammar Station did fairly well on some simple tests, to which I also subjected MS-Word. Neither is perfect.

Below are some responses from Grammar Station. The site divides the results into two types: recommended suggestions (when it's pretty sure of itself) and usage errors (when it knows something is wrong but doesn't know the fix). FYI, 'Your Input' refers to the phrase I provided to Grammar Checker.

Your Input:
You're dog is cute.

(Word saw nothing amiss with this one, but Grammar Station caught the error.)

Recommended suggestion(s) ...
Your dog is cute.

Your Input:
John is to tall for the doorway.

(Both Word and Grammar Station caught this one.)

Recommended suggestion(s) ...
John is too tall for the doorway.

Your Input:
It's a shame that the dog lost it's bone.

(Word missed this one.)

Usage Error(s)...
It is a shame that the dog lost it is bone.

(Grammar Station knew something was wrong, but apparently not how to correct it. When in doubt, contractions are out.)

Then I tried a variation.

Your Input:
Its a shame that the dog lost its bone.

Word corrected this one, but Grammar Station missed it.

Tread warily in the realm of writing. In this age of perceived diminished accountability, the responsibility for correct spelling and proper usage is yours. A machine or a computer program can not replace the human element. It sup two yew.

5

The Look of Appraisal

EYE CONTACT: TO LOOK OR NOT TO LOOK

Eye contact in communication is dicey. A look can be an invitation or an invasion, a challenge or an appraisal. A lot of appraising goes on in Los Angeles.

I flew out there recently from Pittsburgh to visit Diana, a producer friend of mine, whom I hadn't seen in several years. The trip was a combination of research for a script I'm rewriting, meetings with industry people, and catching up on old times. Part of the research was checking out the Hollywood culture.

One evening, we had dinner at the Palm Restaurant, a rustic, semi-pricey watering hole billed as a hangout for celebrities. Diana wanted to check it out as background for the characters in the script. The research started as soon as we walked to our table.

Every now and then, people tell me I look "distinguished." I'm 56 years old, and I choose to believe they mean it and that the phrase is not code for "getting up there." As Diana and I walked to our table, we passed a couple seated in a booth. The young woman looked at me – this is the best adverb I can come up with – thoroughly. It could have been my musky animal magnetism, but more likely she was wondering if I was anybody.

That feeling suddenly went two-way when we were seated in our booth. After I had checked out the more or less identifiable caricatures of movie stars painted on every visible wall, I looked around at the actual people. I saw a young man sitting in another booth diagonally from us with another man whose back was to me. The young man looked familiar: dark hair, movie star looks. I knew he was somebody. Occasionally I darted glances at him, trying to remember his name. The interesting thing is that he kept glancing at me; *he* was trying to figure out who *I* was.

The same thing happened the next evening in the restaurant of the Four Seasons hotel, but with a difference. Diana wanted to show me the famous hotel, so after a charity screening of *A Place in the Sun* at Paramount, we went to the Four Seasons for dessert and coffee.

This was a completely different venue from The Palm: elegantly appointed with a lot of glass and dark wood, subtle lighting, and a nice audio overlay of jazz. As we walked through the bar, I realized the difference from the Palm.

The previous evening, the appraising looks had been subtle and sidelong. Here the looks of some of the patrons are silent, but unmistakably direct, questions: "Who are you and what can you do for me?" (We saw no celebrities at the Four Seasons, but the buttermilk chocolate cake was star quality.)

Of course, not everyone in L.A. stares at other people. It depends on where you are. I had some phone calls to make and writing to do during the day while Diana was at work at Disney, so I found a Borders book store in Sherman Oaks, a few miles from my hotel.

While working on my laptop in the café, I noticed there was no staring or even covert glances by the other customers. True, many of them were doing LA things: one man read a book on being a producer, a woman talked on her cell phone about production values and creative strategies, and another fellow was riffling through pages of a script. But no gawking around and no appraising looks; they were busy. (Apparently, I was the only one gawking.)

The entertainment industry is as competitive as NASCAR, with everyone racing around, trying to inch ahead of the pack, and with a script in the back seat. There are places you go in LA to see and be seen; The Palm Restaurant and the Four Seasons, for instance. Not Borders.

Back to the Palm Restaurant. I finally figured out who that young man was when I got a look at his dinner companion. The young man was John Stamos, and he was having dinner with his *Full House* co-star, Bob Saget. (Now you know: I'll drop a name at the drop of a hat.)

To show you that I'm not star-struck, I won't dwell on the fact that Ray Liotta was on my flight back to Pittsburgh. And I didn't stare.

6

NSW = No Such Word

BE CAREFUL USING WORDS THAT DON'T OFFICIALLY EXIST

Words are used every day that are found in no standard dictionary. These are the NSWs, or no such word. While the use of these "words" might be fun and creative, there will often be a problem with how they're perceived. I'm guessing that many of you will disagree with me on some of the examples. Whether you admit it or remain silent, many of you use these NSWs, either in speaking or in writing. Other NSWs no doubt exist, but the following list comprises the ones that are most noticeable to these editorial eyes and picky sensibilities.

Acrosst. No, the word is *across*. Some of us are afraid to end a word with a hiss. We have to chop it off. I hear the word spoken often enough that I include it, but fortunately have never seen it in print unless it's used in fiction as deliberately substandard dialogue.

Alot. There exists *allot*, meaning to apportion or dole out; and *a lot*, an imprecise way to say a whole bunch. But there exists no such word as *alot.*

Alright. It's in the dictionary, but it's considered substandard, so it makes my list. Stick with the two-word phrase, all right?

Ascared. I'm afraid not. The word is *scared.*

Boughten. Nope, it's *buy, bought, bought.* You might be comparing it phonetically to *get, got, gotten.*

Congradulations. Is this how you say "best wishes" to a graduate? The word is *congratulations.* Incorrect pronunciation leads to incorrect spelling.

Conversate. You can converse or you can have a conversation. Think of another similar word: *Perspiration* doesn't mean you perspirate.

Definately. More a spelling problem than a speaking one, but the correct spelling is definitely not that.

Flustrated. This non-word should perhaps be an actual one, signifying the state of being flustered and frustrated simultaneously. But it isn't yet.

Heighth. Lose the final *h.* The word is *height.* The error is understandable – if not forgivable – because we have such measurement words as *width, breadth, and depth*, not to mention *eighth.*

Hisself. Sounds logical, but remember this is English. The word is *himself.*

Irregardless. This is a non-word that would disappear if its abusers would take a second to consider its supposed meaning. *Ir-* is a negating prefix, *-less* a negating suffix. You don't need both. You might be thinking either of irrespective or regardless.

Mischevious. It's not mis-CHEE-vee-us, it's MISS-che-vus, as in *mischievous*.

Per say. This is an example of phonetic guessing, based perhaps on not having seen the term in writing. *Per se* means "by nature" or "in and of itself."

Pronounciation. I passed a classroom one day and heard an instructor tell her class of future job seekers that, during an interview, correct pro*noun*ciation is very important. Wonder how she got her job. *Pronunciation* is the correct word.

Snuck. The past parochial constrictive of "snack", as in "I didn't want to snack before dinner, but since I had already snuck before lunch, I figured what the hell." Seriously, the preferred verb forms are *sneak, sneaked, sneaked,* although *snuck* is making such definite inroads that it won't be on the list for long.

Theirselves. Use *themselves*. Refer to *hisself*.

Unthaw. Think about it: when you unfreeze a pound of hamburger, you *thaw* it. So if it unthaws, does it re-freeze? Not only is it ungrammatical, it's unsafe food handling.

Whala. It's *voilà* in French. Pronounced "vwah-LA," it means, hey, looky there.

I present this list not to vent (though there is some satisfaction in that), but to help. Inadvertent use of these NSWs lowers your worth and perceived knowledge in the opinion of your listeners and readers. Whether you're in the business or personal world, I want you to sound smart.

All right?

7

This Year, Take Notes

PAY ATTENTION TO YOUR MEMORY TRIGGERS

Memories are very close to the surface this time of year. Part of the reason might be that stress makes us more thin-skinned, but I think the main reason is that there are many more sensory triggers floating around. Decorations everywhere, snatches of song, aromas of baked goods and pine trees, a sip or seven of eggnog, paper cuts from wrapping gifts. All the senses are brought in to play — sight, hearing, smell, taste, and touch — and they all can trigger memories of Christmases past. This year, I suggest you break the tradition of not writing down the memories that surface because of these triggers. Pay attention to your senses. This year, take notes.

Memory triggers are sensual in nature, and often the trigger will be visual. I still have the Lionel train my parents bought for me when I was a year old, and one look at it takes me back to my childhood, especially when it's set up under the tree and surrounded by presents.

The train still works. The growl of the engine sounds exactly the way it did when I was three feet shorter. Over the years, though, the sound of the whistle has deteriorated from a shrill blast to an anemic, gargly coo, but now and then it regains its strength. Turning the wheels of the locomotive by hand and listening to the ratchety buzz of the gears is another trigger.

Just holding the engine in my hand takes me back. The weight and feel of the locomotive is so much different from the other cars, as is the smoothness of the black paint and the slightly raised feel of the engine number 2036 stenciled below the cab's window. It was always a test of strength holding the big engine in my small hand, and trying to get all the wheels aligned on the track.

Then there's the sense of smell, the hair trigger of recall, the hands-down winner in the memory sweepstakes. Years ago, the sharp/sweet tang of the engine oil sailed up my nose and into my brain and took up permanent residence along side those of Necco Wafers and Vick's VapoRub.

We can't ignore the sense of smell. We can turn off some of our other senses, depending on how occupied our minds are. We can ignore the sight of people around us, tune them out when they speak, even ignore the taste of what we're eating. But we can't not smell something.

The train is not a perfect example, because it doesn't involve the sense of taste. Unless I were to load the flatcar with, say, chocolate chip cookies.

I'm making a note to give that a try.

8

Binding Resolutions

RESOLVE TO COMMUNICATE GOODER

Just when you thought you were safe from chatter about resolutions…

Now that the majority of you have let your less relevant New Years resolutions lapse, here's an important one to stick to: resolve to be a better communicator. You can start by not making these common errors in writing and speaking.

Spell minuscule correctly. If you pronounce it correctly, you stand a better chance of spelling it correctly. MIN-***us***-cule, not MIN-***iss***-cule. As a memory device, remember that "minus" is part of the word. If your equation is 5 minus 4 equals 1, the remainder is minuscule compared to the number you started with.

Everyday and every day. I see the misuse of these terms often, even on professionally produced signs and TV commercials. *Everyday* is a one-word modifier that refers to something that happens very frequently, as in every single day. In the phrase *every day*, *every* is the modifier and *day* is the noun. Some people write such things as "I exercise everyday." Wrong. Write instead "I exercise every day" or "For me, exercise is an everyday occurrence." (That's a little wordy, but at least it's correct.) Here's a memory device for you: What if they exercise on alternate days? Would they write "I exercise everyotherday"?

Apostrophes. Do not use an apostrophe to make a singular noun plural. While many a plural noun has an apostrophe, that doesn't make it plural … it makes it possessive. Example 1: *the dog's house.* Here we're talking about one dog with one house. Dog is singular and possessive, made so by adding *'s*. Example 2: *The dogs' houses.* Multiple dogs with multiple houses. First make the dog plural by adding *s*, then an apostrophe. It gets a little dicey when the noun already ends in *s*, as in business. In this case, adding *es* makes it plural: businesses. On the off chance that you want to make businesses possessive, add an apostrophe: businesses'.

Quotation marks. Do not use quotation marks for emphasis. Quotes usually enclose titles, such as songs, stories, and articles, as well as actual quotations. But quotes can also mean irony. A kind of punctuation code for winking. Here's an example you might see in a memo: Remember to bring your "information packet." Any reader with a functioning sense of irony will interpret that phrase as meaning that the packets are not informative at all. Think of "air quotes." If you want to emphasize, underline.

Avoid overcapitalization and overemphasis. Some people cap a word for Emphasis. Not a good idea. Capitalize only proper nouns, titles, and the first word of a sentence. You can indicate emphasis with exclamation points, but you can reach the saturation point quickly. My goodness!!!!!!!! How many of them do we need?!?!?!? Pick emphatic words rather than emphatic punctuation.

Nouns used as adjectives. This insidious problem is creeping into everyday business communication, and it won't be long before it's popping up everywhere. The issue is a problem because it causes confusion. I was once given a document to read with the following title: *Information Literacy Competency Standards in Higher Education.* I hope you enjoyed the irony when you got to the "higher education" part. Note the quotation marks. It's all right to use one noun as an adjective now and then (I did it in the first sentence of this section with the phrase "business communication"), but don't use a whole string of them. Let's try an alternative: *Standards of Competency for Information Literacy in Higher Education.*

Anxious and eager. These words are not synonyms; they have different meanings, at least officially. Anxious means to have anxiety about something; a negative emotion. Eager means (according to dictionary.com) having or showing keen interest, intense desire, or impatient expectancy; a positive emotion.

Less and fewer. Because life is short, I've given up inveighing against the misuse of "less" in the signs at the supermarket checkout that read "12 items or less." But know that the usage is incorrect. If you want to sound smart, follow this rule: Less refers to amount (how much), and fewer refers to quantity (how many). Ex: There is less water in my buckets than in yours, but you have fewer buckets than I do.

Everyone likes agreement… and that includes agreement between parts of speech. Make your modifier agree with your noun. Do not say or write "those kind of things." *Those* is called a demonstrative pronoun, but it's a plural one. *Kind* is singular and that's the word being modified, not *things*. Say "that kind of thing" or "those kinds of things."

You can probably think of other problems in addition to these, but I have resolved to not overburden you.

9

Conventionally Speaking

TRAVELING FOR BUSINESS: ENLIGHTENING AND A PAIN

I flew out to Utah recently to speak at the Genealogy and Family Heritage Jamboree, sponsored by the genealogy group, *My Ancestors Found.* The convention was held at the Dixie Convention Center in the town of Saint George, a quiet little retirement community tucked into the southwestern corner of the state. That part of Utah is beautiful (can't speak for the rest of it; haven't seen it), with its red hills and clear sky; doubly so, because the weather was sunny and quite mild for early February.

I was both a speaker and a vendor, and was thrilled with the turnout. Various estimates were floating around, but at least 800 people attended the wide variety of classes presented during the two days. The huge exhibit hall was open to the public, and estimates of the traffic visiting the vendors' booths were well over 1,000. As one of the 60 vendors, I was in good and appropriate company. The traditional rubbed elbows with the high-tech, with everything available from books on the details of Native American heritage to computer programs for various stages of research. When I was off in a meeting room giving my seminar, the nice folks in *Dear Myrtle's* booth across the aisle watched my booth. In fact, Myrt herself invited me to be a guest on her podcast. (That has since been recorded and is available at dearmyrtle.com)

Because the location was Utah, most of the attendees were members of the Mormon Church (Latter Day Saints, or LDS for short). Everyone was very friendly and pleasant, and at the same time, they take genealogy seriously. One of the attendees told me that the seriousness comes from the fact that researching their ancestors amounts to a religious requirement. Seems like every third person I talked with was either writing a family history or ready to start, so they warmed to the basic idea of my first book: telling your true story using techniques of fiction.

With 60 vendors wade through, however, many of the visitors were suffering from information overload. In order to win raffle prizes, they had to get their vendor sheet stamped, stickered, or initialed by every vendor in order to qualify for the drawings. Because of the way the sheet was laid out, several poor souls wandered up to my booth, handed me the sheet, and dazedly asked, "Have I been here yet?"

If you ever decide to be a vendor at a convention, remember the obvious: everybody likes things they don't have to pay for. My informational handouts and flyers moved like free hotcakes. Something interesting also happened with what the visitors did have to pay for. I sold copies of my book separately and copies of my audio CD set separately, as well as the book/CD combo for a reduced price. Many people bought the book by itself, but others bought the CDs only along with the book. I don't know the reason for that; I'm just throwing it out there. If you have any thoughts as to why this happened, please drop me a line.

The convention itself was pleasant, but the travel was not. Coming back from St. George by way of Los Angeles on Sunday, my flight to Pittsburgh via Newark was cancelled because of a big snowfall in the East. It seems the airlines have this quaint tradition of not letting a plane take off unless they're assured of having a place to land. So I stayed in a nice hotel near LAX for an extra day. At least I thought it would be one day.

That night I started getting chills, and by the next day, I had a full-blown 24-hour bug. So I cancelled my already rescheduled flight, and crawled into bed to watch movies all day, hitting the pause button occasionally to indulge in other less pleasant activities. A word of advice: When you're alone away from home and you get sick, nobody cares.

After other ticket snafus, which I won't bother you with, I finally got home a full two days later than planned. The results of my trip in brief are as follows. Marketing and speaking at the convention: a great experience, enjoyed it thoroughly. Traveling to and from: my garage never looked so good.

10

Shhhh....

KNOW WHEN TO WAIT

Have you noticed how we North Americans dislike conversational silences? Where nature abhors a vacuum, we abhor lulls in a conversation. At the slightest pause, we rush to fill the yawning maw of silence. For the savvy networker or interviewer, this trait can be useful

There's a technique used by television reporters in their stand-up interviews. Picture your TV screen: We see a close-up of the person being interviewed and the reporter's hand holding the microphone in their face. The person finishes the sentence, but the reporter, sensing something else might be coming, remains silent and continues to hold the microphone in front of the interviewee. The poor civilian, not being wise to this trick, assumes more is expected of him, so he says something off the cuff. He blurts. And it's probably more interesting and revealing than what he has already said. Watch for it on your local news. If the editor doesn't cut right after they finish a sentence, you know something more is coming. We see it only if it works, but we see it often.

You can use this technique in a limited fashion in your conversations and interviews. Many a novice has cut off a potentially fascinating answer because the other person paused. Don't be so quick to fill the silence; let your conversational other do it. Pause once in a while to see if there is more to come.

Don't do this every time, or the people you're talking to will think you either dull-witted or a space cadet. Use your common sense, your listening ability, and the other person's nonverbal cues. If you pay attention, you can often read whether or not someone has more to say. Add silence to your conversational toolbox.

11

Telephone v. E-mail

THE EQUILIBRIUM OF ETIQUETTE

Alexander Graham Bell had some brilliant ideas, but how to answer his most famous invention wasn't one of them. Bell wanted to answer the telephone by chirping a chipper "ahoy." Another suggestion, if it had caught on, would have had him answering by saying, "Who wants Bell?" Thomas Edison eventually introduced the idea of saying "hello," and telephone communication was off and running.

Skip forward 100 years. In 1982, Stuart Berg Flexner's *Listening To America* was published. This book is a fascinating study of English terms, sayings, and all manner of interesting uses of our language as it applies to widely varied disciplines, inventions, and walks of life. In the section on the telephone, he writes: "The main change the telephone has made is simply this: it has greatly decreased the amount we write and increased the amount we talk." That was true … in 1982. But we didn't have e-mail then.

Nowadays, we needn't worry about what to say when we answer the phone, because we don't do it. We have a perfectly nice, standard "hello," but do we use it? No. We let the call go to voicemail because we're too busy pecking out e-mails. Could that be why so many voicemail messages go unreturned?

E-mail came into widespread use in the early 90s, and in that time its use has increased dramatically. Any number of census stats and other records show the increase in e-mail usage, but let's look just at the state of Minnesota. During state house sessions, the average number of phone calls legislators received in a week was 47 in 1997; the number rose modestly to 50 a week in 2002. For those same years, e-mails averaged 27 a week in '97 and shot up to 129 in '02. Another sign of the times: the number of actual letters dropped from 29 in '97 to 24 in '02. And that was four years ago; the disparity is surely greater now.

Amid all the numbers, an ironic reversal has taken place. We are now phoning less and e-mailing more, but now we're less equipped for the latter. We had already been writing for more than 5,000 years when Bell said his first "ahoy," but it doesn't take long for writing skills to atrophy. Less than a generation, in fact.

When e-mail first made its appearance, I was heartened. Naively, I thought this new computer technology would be the rebirth of the lost art of letter writing. Sadly, we have not returned to the pre-telephone level of writing, either in quantity or quality, nor will we ever. We now have the technology where the written word could make a comeback, but many of us lack the classic training in the old fashioned skills that accompany letter writing: grammar, spelling, and composition skills. This is not true for everyone, of course, but we have all seen the epidemic of lapses. Little or no punctuation, capitalization is optional, and who has time for Spellcheck?

This state of affairs is as much a result of technology as it is education. E-mail asks of us the composing skills of letter writing, but at the same time it gives us the transmission speed of a phone call. And we get caught up in the speed side of the equation. When you write an e-mail, do you take the time to include a salutation, or do you just plow right in? We're busy, and that's not technology's fault; the speed of e-mail just happens to match the rapid pace at which we think we must accomplish everything else.

We have had more than 120 years to perfect our telephone etiquette. We identify ourselves. We take turns speaking. We say "hello" and "good-bye" … or "buh-bye" if you prefer. (Although there's still that nagging problem of returning voicemails.) E-mail, on the other hand, is too young; in fact it's still evolving. But into what? Will we ever reach a state of etiquette equilibrium with our e-mail messages and phone calls?

Send me an e-mail or give me a call and let me know your experiences and opinions. Or even if you just want to say "ahoy."

12

Personalities in Storytelling

POPULATE YOUR STORIES WITH VIVID CHARACTERS

A story, to use its most elementary definition, is about something happening to someone. But it's also about people interacting with other people. Whether you tell the story as an example in a company presentation or at a family picnic, having an idea of the respective personality types of the people interacting in your stories can help make sense of what happened. And that can help you tell a better story.

Books on personality types abound, so I won't reinvent the wheel. No matter what source you read, the types will usually break down to four. Myers-Briggs compounds the depth by having four distinct characteristics making up each of their types, making a total of sixteen. I'll keep it simple with four, and they're the classic four.

Expanding on the ideas of Aristotle, the Roman physician Galen (second century A.D.) believed that one's personality was governed by the relative amounts of each of the four "humors," or fluids, found in the body. Blood, black bile, choler (yellow bile), and phlegm each correspond to the personality types of sanguine, melancholy, choleric, and phlegmatic.

Sanguines are the party people. You often hear sanguines before you see them, and then when you see them, you can't miss them. They gravitate toward bright colors and lively conversation, lots of people and lots fun. Sanguines make wonderful salespeople because they're so focused on others. Don't look to them for organization skills; they have no time for such details.

Cholerics are the driven drivers. They need to succeed and they need others to follow their way of doing things. Born leaders, cholerics will be sure to get the job done. They might bruise a few feelings along the way since they're looking less at the people involved than at the goal at hand. Interestingly, cholerics can be recognized by their unusually heavy footfalls.

Melancholies are the sensitive organizers. I see melancholy types as contained. No wild clothes or hairstyles or body movements. Where cholerics tread heavily, melancholies glide. Their feelings are easily hurt, so they don't mix well with cholerics. With their tendencies to make lists, they can help sanguines be better organized.

Phlegmatics are the steady and reliable wits. Don't try to argue with a phlegmatic; it won't happen. True phlegmatics strive to avoid conflict by negotiating agreements. Doing this might involve a display of their dry sense of humor. Good detail people, they sometimes focus on the wrong details at the expense of the big picture.

Don't worry if the people in your stories appear to fall into multiple categories. Most people are blends of the four types, but often one or two aspects dominate. Be careful: ascertaining someone's type tends to result in painting a person in broad strokes, resulting in room for error. This technique should be used as a basic classification device, which will result in a clearer picture of the people who populate your stories. Good luck!

13

Where There's A Will...

THERE'S A WAY TO YOUR AUDIENCE

Presentation skills are mandatory homework for speakers, both seasoned and aspiring. You can find inspiration not only from the ranks of professional speakers, but from other professionals on the lecture circuit as well. And take special note of how they handle audiences that might not be completely on their side.

My friend Kim is a subscriber to the Pittsburgh Speakers Series, and she invited me to hear George Will one evening. I was impressed. Will is primarily known as a writer, specifically an author and a conservative political columnist. But he also has media savvy, having been a long-time regular on NBC's *Meet the Press*. During his speech, Will presented his right-leaning views so eloquently, intelligently, and humorously that I almost forgot that I'm supposed to have my apolitical feet firmly planted in the middle of the road.

Will is widely known as a big baseball fan, and he used more national pastime stories than Bob Prince. He gave us such gems as the one about White Sox manager Jeff Torborg taking pitcher Jim Kern out of the game. "But I'm not tired," Kern protested. Torborg replied, "I know, but the outfielders are." Will also quoted Clark Griffith, owner of the lamentable Washington Senators: "Fans like home runs, and we have assembled a pitching staff to please our fans."

At first I didn't think that telling these anecdotes would help Will with this predominantly liberal audience brimming with rabid Steeler fans, but it did for these reasons: he used them at just the right times, and he was very likeable. He was also very smart.

Mr. Will was acutely aware that he was deep in the territory of the Loyal Opposition. Pittsburgh hasn't had a Republican mayor since the 1930s, and Democrats outnumber Republicans here five to one. He was smart to establish his ties to the region, citing his grandfather who was a Lutheran minister in nearby Donora. He was also smart in quoting Democrats such as his late friend, Sen. Daniel Patrick Moynihan, who said, "Everyone is entitled to his own opinion, but he's not entitled to his own facts."

That was one of the points Will emphasized, that facts are facts and can't be manipulated or ignored. He was open about the faulty intel on WMD, and that the war in Iraq is a fatal folly. (My alliteration, not his) The audience approved. They even laughed at his remark about the Republicans' secret weapon in an election year: The Democratic Party.

But the audience was not entirely subservient to celebrity or agreeable to the speaker's *bon mots*. A baseline rumble rippled through the crowd when he endorsed George W. Bush's choices for the Supreme Court. But overall, the audience was respectful.

I'm glad Will couldn't see the reactions of the 60-ish lady sitting next to me. She didn't laugh at any of his jokes, keeping her lips permanently pursed throughout the speech. I guess she was a subscriber to the series and didn't want to waste her ticket, even though she obviously came disposed to disagree.

Trim and fit at 66, Will was rarely behind the lectern, preferring to move about the stage and relate to the audience. He did tend to stay stage right (appropriately), but to be fair, that's where the lectern was. The wandering had no effect on the delivery of the content.

It was content that required the audience to pay close attention in order to keep up. He made his points rapidly, but didn't speak that way. Statistics and examples at his mind's fingertips, he rarely consulted his notes, half a dozen three-by-five note cards. And that's for a 90-minute presentation, mind you.

The only time his delivery understandably faltered was during the question and answer period. The host, a local public radio personality, read some selected questions from cards that had been collected from the audience during the speech. Naturally Will had to stop and think of responses (mostly because some of the questions weren't that well-phrased), and that portion was less smooth. But the audience showed they still liked him when, during one answer, he launched into yet another baseball story. He hadn't even finished his first sentence, and when the audience realized it was a sports analogy, they laughed immediately.

George Will received the classic Pittsburgh reward at the end of the evening: a standing ovation. I don't mean to belittle the gesture, but Pittsburghers give out a lot of those. (At hockey games, local fans give a standing O to the Zamboni driver.) But the gesture still proved that you don't have to tell the audience members what they want to hear in order to get them on your side. You just have to give them the straight facts in a way they can appreciate. And be nice about it.

14

Who Cares ... More or Less?

LET'S FIX A BROKEN EXPRESSION

The story goes that back in 1917, when Congress passed the law instituting Daylight Savings Time, a woman wrote an impassioned letter to the President, pleading with him not to put it into effect. She said that her delicate exotic plants couldn't take the extra hour of daylight.

Common sense dictates that neither human beings nor Congress has a speck of control over the number of hours the sun shines on any given part of the Earth. If Plant Lady had devoted a moment of rational thought to her flora's predicament, she would have realized that her plea made no sense. So it is with the sentence "I could care less."

When someone says "I could care less," logically that means there is still some caring going on. There is, in fact, room to care less. But if one says "I couldn't care less," that means we have reached absolute zero on the concern-o-meter. And that is exactly the intent of the expression.

In his book, *The Language Instinct*, Professor Steven Pinker of MIT, an acknowledged expert on language and the mind, argues that "could care less" is perfectly acceptable because it is intended to convey sarcasm. What the speaker/writer really intends, he says, is an understood reversal of the true meaning, as though it were being said with a rolling of the eyes. I confess that I can't quite wrap my mind around that. Just when I think I can grasp Pinker's meaning, it slips away like fog in a stiff breeze.

Pinker attributes the usage to "young people," but as far back as the mid-1970s, I knew a 50-year-old man who used the same "could care less" expression. I don't believe that people, young or old, devote a lot of spare time to parsing out the intended meanings of expressions. Did a group of confirmed sarcastics get together and decide to wring some irony out of the old saw? Doubt it.

Professor Pinker makes his argument from the sender's perspective; I make mine from the receiver's. To these ears, "could care less" is such a verbal hiccup that I must make a brief extra effort to stay fixed on the content of the message. If you use it in writing, the effects are fixable. Your reader can take as much time as necessary to cluck his tongue or shake her head, then continue reading and not miss a beat. However, if you're a speaker who uses this mal-locution, you risk losing the audience's focus. Besides, many people are irritated by "could care less," and as a result, they might think less of you.

Time to change the clocks soon. Mind those plants.

15

Elusive Answers

DO YOU NEED ALL THE ANSWERS TO GET TO THE REAL STORY?

In my seminars on storytelling, one of the techniques I discuss is using the six questions of a reporter. You know them: who, what, when, where, why, and how. If you ask yourself or others these questions about an event, the answers will give you the informational building blocks to construct a well-told story. But there's one question that might not offer an easy answer, and that's number 5: why.

You should answer all the other questions, or the story will fail. It would be like leaving eggs out of a cake recipe. The cake would bake, but you wouldn't want to eat it. Can the answer to 'why' be left out, and still result in a satisfying story? As an example, I offer an excerpt from the final chapter of my book, *The Stories of Our Days.* (Copyright 2005, reprinted by permission of me.)

"In the late seventies, after graduating from art school with a degree in photography, I worked for a photo lab for little money, so little that I couldn't afford to go away for vacation. My first apartment was in a house with a decent back yard, and that's where I decided to spend the sunny summer days of my week off. The property was surrounded by trees out of which came the twittering of birds, so I figured that counted as communing with nature.

I sat in a lawn chair (because I didn't have a chaise), shirt off, reading and soaking up the sun. The second day of that week, I was sunning and reading when I felt a fluttering on my left shoulder. I turned and pulled my head back as far as I could in order to focus, and I saw a monarch butterfly.

The butterfly simply rested there on my shoulder, wings wafting gently in the light breeze. Ordinarily, I don't like anyone reading over my shoulder, but I was willing to make an exception in this unusual circumstance. I didn't see any reason to brush it away since butterflies aren't poisonous and I had never heard of one sinking its talons into its prey and flying off with it to feast. So we both sunned ourselves. After a while, it fluttered away. "How interesting," I thought. "Nature is communing with me."

The next day was sunny, so I returned to my post in the back yard. Only a few moments after sitting down, I felt a familiar flutter on my shoulder. The same butterfly was back, resting on the same shoulder. So we spent some more time together.

It happened yet again the next day.

Three days in a row. Same back yard, same butterfly, same shoulder.

This is the only story in the book that has no ending, because, to this day, I'm not completely certain what I was being told. If it was a sign, it was a subtle one, because nothing life-altering happened to me around that time. Later I took it as a sign to pay attention to the little things, because they can lead to bigger ones.

I'm still paying attention."

Now let's analyze the ingredients. A story is always about something happening to somebody, so the 'who' is obvious – it's me. 'What' is the fact that a butterfly liked me (call me "the Butterfly Whisperer"). 'When' it happened: a summer day in the mid-seventies. 'Where' it happened: Pittsburgh, Pennsylvania, in the back yard of the house I was living in. 'How' the events played out: a butterfly paid repeated visits to my left shoulder, then went away and I never saw it again.

I had to answer five of the questions; otherwise, my readers would be doing a lot of head scratching. The 'where' and 'when' answers are, in this case, not essential to understanding the events in the story, but the reader feels reassured when a complete picture is presented. But one could spend a sizeable chunk of time pondering the 'why' of this story.

Not being privy to the thought processes of insects, I don't know why that particular butterfly liked me so much. If the writer doesn't or can't answer the question 'why' in recounting an event, is it still a story? The short answer is yes, it is. Part of the ending of this story is my statement that the story has no ending. That's a little tautological, but it serves to illustrate the fact that an important element of a story might be why the event happened in the first place. But an unanswerable question can lead to a story's afterlife.

What makes you remember a certain novel or movie? Often it's the unanswered (or unanswerable) questions that provide the meat for later discussions in the book group or the coffee klatsch after the movie. The other part of the ending to this anecdote is my explanation of the 'why.' Even though I don't have a cut and dried answer, I did reach my own conclusion about why the butterfly came to visit – that it was a sign that I should pay attention to little things. That might not be the right answer, but even if it isn't, my question is "answered" to my satisfaction.

Now don't be tricky and withhold answers simply to prolong the life of your story. If you know the answers, provide them. But if you honestly don't know all the answers, see if the story has legs without them. If the unanswered questions are provocative and your story is still complete, it will live far beyond the time your reader spends on the page.

16

The Truth Is In There

THE TRUTH MIGHT NOT BE OBVIOUS. DIG DEEPER

Do you ever get agitated about something and not know why? Your heart races or your palms sweat, but you can see no obvious reason for these reactions. At this time of year, you might attribute it to getting all scrooged up about the looming holidays or the dearth of daylight. Whatever the cause, something is happening outside of your usual range of vision, something that you should be paying attention to and should probably be writing about.

Constant readers of this column know that I'm an animal lover. (That's "animal," not "animalistic.") I judge the success of walking my daily, three-mile exercise course not by oxygen uptake or target heart rate, but rather by the number of dogs and cats I get to play with en route. Animals like me. So, apparently, do trees.

I wear a sports monitor on these walks. It keeps track of the duration of exercise, average and peak heart rates, as well as heart rate during exercise. (The high-end model gives you real-time stock quotes and doubles as a metal detector.) The monitor's sensor is built in to a strap I wear around my chest, and the digital readouts appear on a sleekly designed wrist watch.

One day, I had to stop to adjust my sock. You know that feeling: a fold develops, and it feels as though someone stuffed a circus tent in your shoe. Bracing one hand on a venerable, two-story-tall elm tree, I lifted my foot and fixed my sock with the other hand. I glanced at my watch and got a surprise: my heart rate was rising.

I'm no expert in sports medicine, but after years of exercising in one form or another, I've learned the elementary fact that heart rate rises during exertion and goes down when you stop. What was going on here? I finished adjusting my sock and took my hand from the elm to get a closer look at the watch. My heart rate had gone up fifteen beats per minute. Then as I watched the readout, my heart rate started to go down. After several seconds, it was nearly back to normal. I touched my hand to the tree again. My heart rate went up again. Hand away, heart rate down. Very interesting.

Now here's something even more interesting, something that seems to raise fundamental questions about our relationship to nature. I placed one hand on the tree, and my heart rate went up. Then I placed *both hands* on the tree; my heart rate went back *down*. With only one hand on the tree, was energy coming into me and couldn't get out? And with both hands on the tree, was I completing a circuit? I don't have an answer yet. Has anyone out there had a similar experience? Or even if you haven't, try it and tell me what happens.

(By the way, I've tried this experiment on many occasions. The phenomenon always occurs with that particular elm tree and most times with most other trees.)

When you feel yourself getting worked up and you're not working out, look around, then look within. Something is happening. The cause might be as simple as too much caffeine, or it could be a fragment of underdone psychic potato or a blot of emotional mustard buried in a deep stratum of yourself that has gone too long ignored. Or the feeling could be coming from a completely natural but unknown source, like a lonely elm tree. You might not find the reason right away, but pay attention. An answer will come. Write it down.

17

Pictures into Words and Vice Versa

PICTURES HAVE THE POWER TO INSPIRE YOU AND HELP YOUR WRITING

You can write about an event until you're blue in the fingers, but sometimes a picture does a lot of the work for you. The words might even take second place, supporting the dramatic, emotional, or humorous effects of the visual element. So it is with the photograph you see here.

This particular event was the fortuitous assembly of deer, wild turkeys, and pet cat all in one place. I captured this image in my back yard in the South Hills of Pittsburgh, Pennsylvania, which is classically suburban, but with a healthy amount of wooded area nearby. Hence, the wildlife.

In this photograph, as with any photograph, you can see only what was happening for the fraction of a second that the shutter was open. But it's what you can't see that requires narrative support.

While this is a typical day in my back yard in that deer and turkeys visit regularly, it's atypical with respect to the lucky confluence of deer, turkeys, and housecat. They usually don't all show up at the same time.

Along with the information your images impart, be aware of the possible emotional reactions of your readers. This photograph will elicit varying reactions depending on the viewers' feelings toward their own local fauna. The only thing many people will see in the photo are pests that munch on their hostas and deposit unwanted fertilizer all over their landscaping.

Me, I like them, both bird and beast. My cat Lulu does too, although the feeling was not mutual; the deer were afraid her. Whenever she moved, the deer snorted and scuttled away, then trotted back to stare. Amazing: young, healthy deer the size of ponies spooked by a 17-year-old tortoiseshell tabby. The turkeys were, as usual, oblivious. You cannot get all that information from one photograph. You need words as backup.

Sometimes, a photograph inspires you to write about it. This one, for instance. I doubt that I would bother to tell you about a bunch of animals wandering around my yard if the photograph weren't so striking (if I do say so myself).

And sometimes the reverse happens: you want to write about something and need a photograph to enhance the impact of your words. Say, your child's wedding. Your main goal is to tell stories leading up to and including the grand event. The photos, good as they may be, should serve only as backup. The main thrust is the event, not the visual record of it.

Where do pictures fit in to your storytelling? If you're a scrapbooker, you're probably more focused on the images, so the words will more than likely serve as captions. If you're a genealogist, you're focused on the stats and stories of your ancestors, so the photographs that still exist will act as support for your words. Let your unique situation dictate the proper place for visuals. You're the best judge.

18

Profiling Your Audience

REACH YOUR AUDIENCE WITH CONTEXT-CENTERED CONTENT

You're a presenter with a message that's appropriate for a wide cross section of society. Do you provide the same basic message to every audience? You should. Do you use exactly the same content, terminology, and methods? You shouldn't. Make your level of discourse match the level of your audience. You can accomplish this by using the concept of high and low context based on your audience's education, experience, and background.

A high-context message leaves much unsaid. The sender assumes that the receiver already possesses essential background knowledge that needn't be spoken. That's how you present to experts. On the other hand, a low-context message is loaded with information, much of it fundamental. That's how you present to beginners.

Pinning down the demographics of a given audience is difficult. The education level of an audience could be uniform or it might vary. If they're all doctors or lawyers or engineers, you can assume much formal schooling, but you don't always get such homogeneous audiences. Experience refers to experience with your particular topic. Be it brain surgery or barbecuing, the respective practitioners will have varying levels of expertise. Background refers to cultural origins, and not just nationality but the part of the country they come from.

Be aware of other factors as well, such as age, gender, and religion. Because these factors can be so different from one audience to another, you need to watch your cultural references. Retirees don't know who the Pokemon characters are, and a lot of pre-teens have never heard of the Beatles.

One of my communication seminars covers how to write a proper e-mail. But I wouldn't provide the same information about grammar and usage to journalists as I would to, say, engineers, doctors, or lawyers. I would use high context with journalists and low context with the others. In fact, there is an entire language section of the seminar that I completely scuttle when I talk to professional wordsmiths because low-contexting them would be insulting. They already know that the words "comprise" and "of" don't belong together, "irregardless" is not a word, and neither is "alot." (At least most of them do.) But facts like these could be enlightening to audiences comprising people who are well educated but whose jobs do not deal primarily with writing. It's not about general intelligence, but about specific knowledge.

The concept of context also applies to books and magazine articles about a specific subject. Photography, for instance. The beginner needs information on the basics: Why is there no film in my digital camera? Where is the shutter release? How do I turn my camera on? The more advanced photographer wants more advanced information: Synchronizing the shutter with electronic flash. Controlling depth of field. Working with backlighting. The tyro would be totally at sea trying to read an advanced article and the expert would be bored with a beginner's topic.

Context can also be used for less-than-honest purposes. As a former teacher, I remember getting papers from students written in high context style. Students are famous for underexplaining a concept they're not sure of. They write the paper in high context thinking the ploy will hide their lack of knowledge. But the teacher wants low context so as to be able to tell whether the student understands the information. (Note to students: We're on to you.)

Context is governed by culture. Japan is an example of an entire society that, in general, communicates in the opposite way from those in the U.S. and Europe. The Japanese style of communication is considered high context. Much information in a message is already understood based on history, tradition, and the desire to maintain harmony.

The Japanese believe that any reasonably intelligent person should be able to carry on a high context conversation. The less one says, the smaller the chance of causing offense and, as a result, making both participants lose face. We on the other hand are low context communicators because so much of our messages are information-based, and if we were to use the high context style, too little information would be transmitted.

You won't always have an audience whose members all have the same education, experience, and background. But you will often have audiences of people who share similar qualities. Address those similarities with context-centered communication, and your message will get through.

19

Everyday Eloquence

THE POWERFUL WORDS ARE NOT ALWAYS THE BIG ONES

Mark Twain wrote, "The difference between the almost right word and the right word is really a large matter—it's the difference between the lightning bug and the lightning." But that lightning can come in a bottle; eloquence can be a small thing.

World War II. Bastogne, France in December of 1944. The Germans demanded that U.S. Army General Anthony McAuliffe surrender his surrounded division at the Battle of the Bulge. The general's defiant reply: "Nuts!"

It has been said that oratory is the art of making deep noises from the chest sound like important messages from the brain. Many of us equate eloquence with Elmer Gantry intensity and hyperbolic, sesquipedalian verbosity. Maybe it's because of the inventory available to us. Consider this: the French language has fewer than 100,000 words. German has around 185,000. In contrast, the Oxford English Dictionary lists around 500,000 words. We have half a million words to choose from, but we don't need to use all of them. Sometimes, though, the big words do provide the bonus of being economical. For instance, I just used the phrase "hyperbolic, sesquipedalian verbosity" (3 words) to impart the idea of "using inflated or exaggerated terms in the form of words with many syllables" (13 words).

Those three words are longer than usual and a trifle uncommon, yet they are precise. Precision of meaning is a prerequisite for eloquence. One source of that precision is the shades of meaning provided by those half million words in the OED. Consider the possible verbs we can call into action to describe "the act of requesting information." If you want to know what time it is, you "ask" the guy who has a watch. If his watch looks suspiciously like one you own but can't find, you might ratchet up the intensity and "question" the person as to where he acquired his timepiece. If you're sure he stole your watch, call the police and let them "interrogate" the miscreant.

Big words can be used with eloquence as the result, but it's not a given. Ten-dollar words do not ensure eloquence, yet the fifty-cent words can galvanize an entire nation. In 1940, Winston Churchill gave a radio address to the people of England about the threat from Germany. He said: "We shall not flag or fail. We shall go on to the end. We shall fight in France, we shall fight on the seas and the oceans, we shall fight with growing confidence and growing strength in the air, we shall defend our island, whatever the cost may be. We shall fight on the beaches, we shall fight on the landing grounds, we shall fight in the fields and in the streets, we shall fight in the hills; we shall never surrender." No ten-dollar words here; they're all effective, no-nonsense fifty-centers. And they work.

Churchill may have chosen these words for a specific reason. In their book, *The Story of English*, Robert McCrum, William Cran, and Robert MacNeil tell us that every word of Churchill's speech is of Anglo-Saxon origin except for two: confidence and surrender. The theory is that the English citizens would respond on a deeper level to words that match their heritage.

William Faulkner once disparaged Ernest Hemingway's writing style by saying that Hemingway "had never been known to use a word that might send the reader to the dictionary." Hemingway's response: "Poor Faulkner. Does he really think big emotions come from big words? He thinks I don't know the ten-dollar words. I know them all right. But there are old and simpler and better words, and those are the ones I use." Why? Why use the old and simple words? Because there is less chance for misunderstanding. There can be no alternative interpretation of Churchill's words. He was saying: We will fight the enemy to the end … anywhere.

Many people hold a negative opinion (or think they do) of eloquence and of public speaking in general. Ben Franklin said: Here comes the orator with his flood of words and his drop of reason. Unfortunately, we have all heard speeches wherein the presenter uses many words to say next to nothing. Use only as many words as you need. The important thing here is picking the right words for your audience.

In Ambrose Bierce's *The Devil and Daniel Webster*, the famed lawyer and orator defended a farmer who had sold his soul to the devil. After arguing with the devil while passing a jug back and forth in the farmer's kitchen, Daniel found himself arguing his case right then and there. The devil had hand picked his jury of damned souls, all of whom, he was sure, would find in his favor. The jury trooped into the kitchen and listened to Daniel Webster's defense. Dan'l took that jury and made them remember what it was like to be alive and human.

...and to each one of that
jury he spoke of things long forgotten. For his
voice could search the heart, and that was his
gift and his strength. And to one, his voice was
like the forest and its secrecy, and to another
like the sea and the storms of the sea; and one
heard the cry of his lost nation in it, and another
saw a little harmless scene he hadn't remem-
bered for years. But each saw something.

And they found for Dan'l Webster. Dan'l knew his audience, and he knew what would move them.

Churchill once said: Short words are best, and old words, when short, are best of all. So if someone tells you that you need big words to impress your audience, just look him in the eye and say … "Nuts!"

20

First-Time Speakers: Get Ready To Goof

MISTAKES ARE PART OF LEARNING

Remember the opening to "The Lone Ranger," all galloping horses and rousing music? My first attempt at speaking led me to wish for escape music and a horse so I could get out of there. If you're thinking of speaking, be warned: get the first time over with, move on, and learn.

Return with us now to those thrilling days of yesteryear, March of 1978, and my first day of teaching. Even though I was a tenderfoot at speaking in front of a group, I figured I could handle it. I handled it, but not well.

I had just gotten a job as a photography instructor at the Art Institute of Pittsburgh. In those days, classes at AIP were day-long events, four hours in the morning, an hour for lunch, and two hours in the afternoon. I prepped for days for that Intro to Photography class, and walked in that morning with eight or ten legal pages jammed with notes. At 8:00 I took roll and then started to teach photography.

I waxed eloquent about the basics of light and shadow, black & white photography as an abstract medium, even alluding to Cartier-Bresson's "decisive moment." I had them in the palm of my hand ... for about 20 minutes. That's how long it took me to go through my notes.

You probably know that feeling of dismayed surprise when your stomach suddenly does a spot-on impression of a clenched fist. That's what I felt when I lifted the last page of notes to see nothing but a vast expanse of yellow paper with those pale green lines. *Empty* pale green lines.

Let's do the math. Twenty minutes into a six-hour class meant I had five hours and 40 minutes left to vamp. Fortunately, I knew my subject, so I was able to go nervously and haltingly off-book. Good thing too, since I had no book left. Another fortunate occurrence was one blessed student bringing back a Life magazine after lunch. I practically grabbed it out of his hands and started critiquing the magazine's photographs for the afternoon session. Somehow I got through the day.

What can we learn from this? Number one: Talk. More. Slowly. That first day I was about as effective as a color-blind paint mixer because I ran through those notes barely taking a breath. (Remember that fast-talking announcer in the old Fed-Ex commercials? He was normal speed compared to my fast forward.) Most beginning speakers think they're talking too slowly and want to pick up the pace. The pace is already up, trust me. Slow down.

Another speed-related concept to remember is that your audience likes pauses. When you take a breath up there and glance at your notes, it's not really as long a gap as you think it is. The respite gives your audience a chance to think about what you've said, even giving them the opportunity to take notes and think of questions.

That's another thing I learned: encourage the audience to participate. Audience interaction, when you're lucky enough to get it, can give you an energy boost and invigorate your presentation. Let them respond to your statements. You might even get a nice discussion going, as long as you maintain control.

I imagine I had very little control of the room in those days. I was only 28 then, not much older than my students, so it's safe to say I was lacking gravitas. I thought that meant that I had to get by on expertise alone. It wasn't until later that I allowed my personality to do some of the work.

That's the third point: let the real you shine through. Whatever you have going for you - expertise, humor, people skills - let that come out. Humor grew to be a large part of my teaching style then, just as it's a large part of my speaking style today. But it was a long time before I was comfortable enough to allow that to happen.

A few years later, a student said something that really cinched the idea of personal style when he compared me to another instructor. He told me that, at the beginning of the semester, he thought I was going to be stuffy and boring and that the other instructor was going to be funny and cool. After he saw my teaching style along with the other guy's, he said his opinion was now just the opposite. It's good to be the cool one.

You also need to closely observe your audience. Watch for signs that they don't understand you or are losing interest. I couldn't tell you whether those students on my first day were with me or not because I wasn't paying any attention to them. I was too busy getting through the material.

Seasoned speakers know the importance of making eye contact with members of the audience because it serves two purposes: it lets the audience know that you're interested in them, and it lets you know whether they're interested in you! It's called feedback. Watch for it.

I did come back the next day and for 25 years after that. I grew to love teaching because I could tell my students were learning from me just as I learned so much from them. Even though my teaching days are over, I'm still speaking in front of audiences large and small, and getting energy and inspiration from them as they get information and inspiration from me. I echo master storyteller Doug Stevenson, who says to his crowds, "I'm one of the weird ones. I like it up here."

You might mess up in your first attempt at speaking, just as I did. Suck it up and try again. Who knows, you might be one of us weird ones and actually get to like it up there.

21

Traditions and Memories

TRADITIONS MIGHT CHANGE, YET THEY ENDURE

Summer will come late this year because there was no Memorial Day. No, don't check your calendar; as I write this, the summer solstice hasn't happened yet. And yes, there was indeed a Memorial Day. But it wasn't "Memorial Day."

The end-of-May holiday has always been a signifier for me. Even though I haven't had an entire summer off in 40 years, Memorial Day still kicks off the season in my head. While it's true that in my grade school years we went back to classes for a few days after Memorial Day, we all knew they didn't count. School was over. Summer was here.

Since before I was born, Memorial Day meant visiting the farm of a distant cousin of my father's to celebrate Aunt

Bessie's birthday. She wasn't really an aunt, but it was easier for a kid to understand.

The event was a sort of combined family picnic/ annual reunion with forty or fifty people showing up with all manner of foods and desserts. Good old American food like stuffed cabbage and sauer kraut and kielbasa, as well as actual American foods like baked beans and potato salad. It was a big deal for me because with rare exceptions, I got to see the country cousins only once a year, even though we lived only a few miles away.

That once-a-year-aspect is probably what made the trip to the farm stand out. That and the different way of life. At home, I had a nice back yard, maybe a couple hundred square feet. At the farm, the "back yard" was 40 acres. At home I had a dog. At the farm, there were hunting dogs and cows and chickens and a pony and deer in the woods and beavers in the stream building their dam. You know ... country stuff.

Not to wring all the juice out of a cliché, but times certainly were different. I remember riding to the farm one year with Mom and Dad in the late 50s right after the town parade. Along the way, my dad picked up a soldier walking along the road carrying his duffle. I remember his uniform was brown, so he might have been a Marine. We dropped him off a few miles along the road and he thanked us. He was friendly and polite and it seemed just right to give a ride to a soldier who was home on leave on Memorial Day.

Aunt Bessie died a generation ago, but fortunately everyone decided to keep the tradition going. We've been having that picnic for more than 60 years now. It's evolved over time. New relatives coming and going and others moving away. Kids being born and oldsters passing on. But the tradition stays.

Traditions can spring up within traditions. Remember the beaver dam I mentioned? At some time during the day - usually after the softball game - a select few would take a walk to see the dam. I took the walk every year and don't remember ever seeing a beaver. Sometimes there wasn't even a dam. The stream is probably half a mile from the farmhouse, all downhill. That meant the walk back was all uphill. Obviously, over the years, fewer and fewer people made the trek because of advancing age. Now no one does. No one plays softball anymore either.

Traditions are strong symbols. Miss one and you might think it doesn't matter. But deep down it does. I have missed only four Memorial Day picnics, and that was when I was in the navy from '68 through '72. Times were busy for the military in those years, but when the day came, I always took a moment to try to transport myself to the farm. It never worked.

Tradition and force of habit are similar. When you fulfill a habit, you don't necessarily feel better, but you'd sure feel worse if you didn't. I'm not talking about funky chemical habits or nicotine satisfaction; I'm talking about holidays and birthdays and getting your favorite table in the café so you can write better. (Or is that just me?) Take the time to write about your own traditions, whether they're still happening or not.

I don't know yet why the picnic was postponed until July 1st this year, and it doesn't really matter. The grandsons of Aunt Bessie kept the farm in the family, and the good folks will still have the picnic. Summer will come, just a little late.

22

Memory Calisthenics

THE FARTHEST YOU'LL EVER TRAVEL WHILE STAYING PUT

It's exercise time, so sit down and close your eyes. What kind of low-impact exercise is this? you might ask. Memory exercise, that's what. Read the article, and then try the procedure later. Maybe you can have someone read this to you as you sit relaxed with your peepers shut.

Find a quiet place and close your eyes. Mentally put yourself in the place you want to describe. Take yourself back there. Or rather, allow yourself to go back there.

You could try playing music from the era because that can help transport you to that other time and place. But be careful of the musical choices; you can't always control what memories will be awakened by a particular song. They could be undesirable ones and distract you from the task at hand. Or the music could open some long-closed doors. I'll leave that to you.

Now that you've remembered a place, it's time to exercise. You've probably heard the term "mind's eye." Well, we're going to use your mind's eyes, ears, nose, tongue and skin. In other words, the senses of your mind.

Experience this place. Include still and moving objects and living things.

*What do you see? What colors? What movement?
*What do you hear? Music? Machinery? Voices? Traffic?
*What do you smell? Animals? People? Perfume?
*What do you taste? Apple pie? Sour milk?
*What do you feel? I'm talking tactile, not emotional. The surface of your skin, not your emotions.

Now take it a step further. In your mind, look under furniture and behind doors. Big photographs are stored behind dressers all the time. Who's in the photographs?

Look under the beds. In your mind's eye, get down on your mind's hands and knees. Mind those mind's dust bunnies. You'll find plenty of shoes. And more lost toys are found under beds than in toy boxes. (That's a long-standing, proven statistic I just made up.)

Open closet doors and see if you remember what's inside. Once you're in there, take inventory. Whose clothes are in there? Your parents'? Your grandparents'? Yours? Open the shoe boxes. Search through pockets. Granted, this part of the exercise borders on fantasy, but it could unearth a nugget. What do you hear under the surface noises? Are there background noises?

Your place can be pleasant or unpleasant, from a country kitchen to a fetid jail cell. (I've experienced only one of those.) From your own cozy bedroom to a fleabag so rank even the cockroaches were jumping out the windows. Let your mind take you. What you record should not be a story, just impressions. The stories will come from the impressions.

The article in the last issue described a pleasant place, the farm of relatives on Memorial Day. This month, we'll go the opposite direction: the engine room of a destroyer from my time in the navy. What do I experience when I close my eyes?

I see mounds of machinery, from enclosed turbines to big, whining generators. Off-white bulkheads coated with dirt. All lit by overhead incandescent bulbs that lent a warm glow to an otherwise soulless environment.

I hear the combined whine-roar of machinery and little else. Any voices I hear have to be filtered from the engine noise.

I smell fuel oil, human sweat, bad coffee, and whatever nameless muck is found in the bilges.

The smell of hot oil is so strong, I could taste it on my tongue. I remember the water cooler. (Some of the guys from other parts of the US called it a bubbler.) And I say cooler with tongue in cheek. The thing mixed room temperature water with water from a cooled reservoir inside. But the reservoir held only about a cup of cold water. So it didn't take long for cool water to be replaced by room temperature water. And room temperature in a fired up engine room was damn hot. Not very refreshing.

I feel deck plates underfoot with their raised elongated diamond pattern. Coating of dirt and oil on them. Don't fall. I feel heat. That reminds me: my first day on board, a first class petty officer, a man named Frey, showed me around the engine room. All the machinery was running and the place was steamy hot. At one point, he stopped and he explained something to me, probably the steam cycle. I realized later that he stopped and told me these things in the hottest part of the space. He turned out to be a nice guy, but that was just part of the initiation.

My overall impression: The place was physically hot, but emotionally cold. After all, it was machinery.

All right, enough of that place. I'm back.

Try this method sometime and write or call with your results. I've shown audience members how to do this during my seminars, and I wish you could see the expressions on their faces when they open their eyes. It's a mix of excitement at what they experienced and sadness that it's over. But it won't be over if you record it before you forget it.

Now close your eyes. Have a nice trip.

23

Lulu Catches a Chipmunk...

AND PROVIDES A LESSON IN PROBLEM SOLVING

It was a red-letter day for catdom. After 18 years of trying, my cat Lulu finally caught her first chipmunk ever. Actually, it's the first time she's caught *anything* ever. The episode illustrates the difference in methods of problem-solving between animals and humans.

(I wish I could tell you that the photograph opposite depicts Lulu stalking her prey, but it doesn't. All it does is show her doing two of her best things: roaming the yard and ignoring the turkeys.)

In all the years Lulu has allowed me to share various lodgings with her, certain small animals have crossed her path and until now all have escaped unscathed. Even this recent catch survived, what scathing there was being confined to emotional trauma, the poor thing.

But this lack of success is not for want of trying on Lulu's part. It could be the fact she has no front claws and dull teeth, but I'm the one who has always had to catch and release. And I had to do it on this day, too. Eventually.

In a nutshell here's what happened:

* Lulu is sniffing around the little holes in the ground near the tree stump where she has stalked chipmunks in the past.

* I'm standing on the patio with my other cat, Fleck.

* Suddenly a flurry of activity attracts our attention: Lulu hurries from behind the stump and strides purposefully toward the open patio door, holding a very much alive chipmunk in her mouth.

* I'm so stunned that I let her get past me and into the house.

* Here she promptly drops Chip (or Dale, I can never remember which is which) and it runs down the hall and into the bathroom and all three bedrooms, both cats in hot pursuit.

* I finally corral the beast in a back bedroom and close the door. Between me and the cats, we still can't catch it.

I made other fruitless attempts at evicting the guest, including buying a humane trap and even building a makeshift ramp to a window. This went on for a couple of hours, so Lulu and Fleck's hot pursuit eventually froze over. In fact, they each took a nap, Lulu downstairs in the office and Fleck on the living room couch.

Finally a cooler head prevailed. I left the chipmunk's bedroom and closed the door. I closed every door on that floor of the house except one: the patio door. I then opened the chipmunk's bedroom door and shooed it out.

The chipmunk high-tailed it down the hall, hung a hard right at the living room, and zipped through the dining room and out the patio door. From the couch, Fleck saw it run by, and she raced out the door after it. Fortunately, she didn't catch it.

Mission accomplished (and not in the banner-decorating-an-aircraft-carrier sense). But the episode raises a question: follow one's first instinct or think the problem through?

Problems arise often in both business and personal life, and that's no grand revelation. It's how we deal with the problems that tests our mettle. When a problem pops up, my customary response is to throw money at it. This is me being proactive.

To my credit, spending money was not my first reaction to the chipmunk. My first try was almost the same as the cat's: chasing it. I donned a pair of work gloves and tried to catch it manually. (Don't scoff, I've caught mice that way.) It didn't work this time. Apparently my reflexes have slowed more than Lulu's.

The second idea was to buy the trap, which I baited with critter feed. That idea bombed. I knew - but didn't think of - the fact that the last thing a panicky animal cares about is lunch, so the trap was not an attraction. I was later able to return it to the hardware store.

Once when I opened the door to check on the guest, it was on the bed looking longingly at the window. ('Longingly' might be too strong a descriptor, but it was looking.) So I got a long piece of wood from the garage, opened the window and removed the screen, and built a crude ramp from the bed to the window. After waiting a while, I found that hadn't worked either. At that point, I opted for Occam's Razor.

No, I didn't try to fillet the little guy. The precept of Occam's Razor is this: don't overcomplicate. In a situation where both a complicated and a simple answer to a problem might exist, the simpler answer is right. So I decided to direct the chipmunk instead of catch it.

The simplest way worked. After two or three hours of buying and building and generally overthinking the problem, the simplest way took less than a minute to succeed.

It took Lulu 18 years to catch her chipmunk because all she has to work with is instinct. She knows only one way to catch something: chase it. She didn't just follow her *first* idea, she followed her *only* idea.

Maybe I was following my first instinct, too, by chasing the critter. After all, I come from a long line of hunter- gatherers, and instincts die hard, if at all. But the thing about *homo sapiens sapiens* is our ability to go beyond instinct to the realm of "what-if." And "what-if" solved the problem.

Disclaimer: Before you castigate me for having Lulu declawed, I offer this in my defense: 18 years ago, I didn't know the exact procedure. Now I do. Fleck has all her claws and she always will.

By the way, I checked. Dale is the one with the red nose and topknot, so Lulu caught Chip. Keep trying, and you'll catch your chipmunk. Just don't overthink.

24

Cultivating Organic Humor

IF YOU USE HUMOR, MAKE IT FIT THE SITUATION

Humor is a funny thing. Everyone thinks they have a sense of humor, but not everyone is right. You can be an effective speaker even if you don't have a sense of humor, as long as you don't try to fake it. (The audience can always tell.) On the other hand, even if you have been blessed with a good sense of humor, you need more than that to be a speaker; you also need a sense of timing. A sense of humor allows you to see the funny aspects of everyday life and the funny relationships between unrelated things. A sense of timing lets you talk about them in a funny way.

We all know what's funny, but we laugh at wildly different examples. One theory says that some nationalities are funnier than others, but I don't buy it. I'm German by ancestry and

I've been known to be amusing, even though you'd probably be hard pressed to come up with a good example of German hilarity. Sure, we have lederhosen and yodeling, but they don't count because we were serious about those. You might ask how on earth we could be serious about such cultural oddities. I answer with another German tradition: beer.

When aspiring speakers ask me if they can open their presentation with a joke, I suggest that they use humor instead. The term 'joke' hits me as being stand-alone and unrelated to a topic or theme. Effective humor is always organic, blending seamlessly with the topic and the audience.

Are isolated jokes funny? Sure they are. The vaudeville comedian Henny Youngman was famous for his disconnected one-liners. "My wife dresses to kill. She cooks the same way." But funny isn't the only criterion; for humor to work within a presentation, it has to be effective, appropriate, and supportive of the topic. You know – organic. Unrelated one-liners don't fit the definition. Besides, being able to tell a joke does not necessarily mean you have a good sense of humor; maybe you just have a good memory.

Organic humor is most effective when it's woven into a story. But for the humor to work along with the point of the story, you really have to know the story. Really know it. REALLY. Pittsburgh radio personality and storyteller Jack Bogut says that a good speaker practices a story until he gets it right. A professional speaker practices a story until he can't get it wrong. For any story – humorous or otherwise – to be effective, it must be told properly and flawlessly, and timing plays a major role.

This assumes you've mastered the basics, such as structure (beginning, middle, and end), progressive disclosure (what details you reveal and when you reveal them), and judicious use of dialogue and description. But it also includes minute details like the choice of language and the rhythm of the words. It isn't only poetry and song lyrics that have rhythm; so do prose and the spoken word.

Let's say you want to make a specific point using a humorous story as an illustration. Here's one for you. As I write this column, the state of New Mexico is unveiling (if that's the right word) a series of public service announcements for the tipsy male from an unusual source: the urinal. Talking urinal cakes will spout messages in a female voice, such as the following: "Hey, you! Yeah, you! Having a few drinks? Then, listen up! Think you've had one too many? Maybe it's time to call a cab or call a sober friend for a ride home. It's sure safer and a hell of a lot cheaper than a DWI! Make the smart choice tonight. Don't drink and drive!"

(I don't know what you would illustrate with this story. That's your problem.)

The article I read didn't say how the talking urinal cakes are activated and I don't want to know. But a Department of Transportation spokesman is quoted as saying that the device is a great idea because it's guaranteed to get "ten or fifteen seconds of undivided attention."

Wait a minute. If you're in a bar restroom and you can take care of business in ten or fifteen seconds, well, you're just not doing your part.

And there's another problem. If the poor guy is really swacked and he's in there all by himself and suddenly hears a woman's voice coming out of the urinal … well, let's just hope he's not wearing sucdc shoes..

Worst case scenario: there's a whole bank of urinals, each with its own babbling deodorizer, all being used at the same time. The cacophony could drive a man to drink.

Notice that each of my comments on the story ends in a one-syllable word. That isn't essential every time, but it's more effective, and it helps the rhythm. Find an amusing story in the newspaper or notice something funny at work, then see what else it makes you think of. How much funnier can you make real life?

While Henny's one-liner would not fit into a speech or presentation, it offers some valuable examples of structure and rhythm. This joke has two parts, the setup and the snapper. "My wife dresses to kill. She cooks the same way." The setup has six syllables and the snapper has five, making only 11 syllables in the whole joke. And every word but one has only one syllable. That's tight and economical writing.

Let's try it another way: "My wife dresses to kill. You could say the same thing about her cooking." It makes the same point, but not as well. Too many words and too many syllables. Plus the second sentence doesn't match the staccato rhythm of the first. In my bad example, I waited until the final word to reveal exactly what is being compared to dressing, and that can be effective. But cooking has one syllable too many. Pay attention to the rhythm. A one-syllable word has more punch, especially if it's the last word.

Many audiences expect a presenter to attempt humor. If the presenter is not a professional speaker, they're also expecting the attempt to be lame. Surprise them.

25

Remember That? Maybe You Do ... Maybe You Don't

YOUR MEMORY CAN PLAY TRICKS ON YOU

Holidays and parties are times for family and friends to get together for food, drink, and – most important – telling stories. But before you tell them, double check your details.

We were discussing memories in one of my memoir writing seminars, and an audience member, Heather, told a fascinating story. Heather remembered going on a car trip when she was very young, with her mother, her father, her brother, and an elderly friend of her mother's, Mrs. Klieger. She told of being in the back seat with her brother and Mrs. Klieger while her mother sat next to her father, who was driving.

Everyone in the back seat was dozing when her mom decided she was hungry and was going to eat some Concord grapes. With the car tooling along the highway, her mom began eating her grapes and spitting the seeds out the open window. Nice idea except for the fact that the rear window was also open and the slipstream carried the seeds right back into the car. Heather remembered waking up to find the sleeping Mrs. Klieger's brilliantly white blouse peppered with purple grape seeds.

It was a funny story, well told, with good visuals. But the fascinating part of the story is the fact that Heather wasn't there.

She told us that years later she related the story in front of her brother, who informed her, "We weren't on that trip." She had told that story for years, mistakenly believing that she and her brother had been occupying the back seat of the car.

Three possible reasons exist for this phenomenon: Heather said that she and her brother always went places with her parents and she probably couldn't fathom being left behind. Another possibility is that she'd heard the story retold so many times at a young age that she inserted herself into it. The third possible reason is the visual quality of the story. The image of purple dots marring a white blouse is easy to visualize, so it's just as easy to imagine being there. The events of the story are indeed true. They transpired as Heather said they did; she just wasn't there to witness them.

So be careful: What you remember might be true, but the details might not.

26

Sense and Nonsensibility

OVERUSED WORDS AND PHRASES

I wrote a paragraph of nonsense and it was published in a newspaper. That might not seem surprising when you consider the editorial content of some of our daily periodicals, but in my own defense and that of the newspaper's, the nonsense was requested.

Samantha Bennett, a humor columnist for the *Pittsburgh Post-Gazette*, issued a challenge to the readers of the P-G to write a paragraph containing their pet peeves in the form of irritating clichés and overworked catchphrases. Using such terms as vile and wretched in her introduction, she published several of the best offenders a week later over a span of two days. Mine made the second cut, and not just because Samantha is a friend of mine. My paragraph was as vile and wretched as the rest of the lot. Judge for yourself.

To Staff: It goes without saying that we must prioritize our paradigms with an end to leveraging the value-added synergy to our best advantage. That's half the battle when opening that can of worms. For continued success moving forward, we must downsize our liabilities, upsize our skill sets, and supersize our viable alternatives. I want to spend quality time picking your brain re: belt-tightening in relation to our at-risk human resources. Let's touch base and plan some face time to craft a mission statement for getting these tasks in the pipeline. Failure is not an option. Thank you in advance for your cooperation in this matter.

Coincidentally (not ironically), Jan Freeman, in her *On Language* column (since rechristened *The Word*) in the New York Times Magazine, addressed the same problem the following Sunday, but with a twist. Why, she asks, does something have to be "wrong" with the original word or phrase that is being replaced by the stressed out neologism? You can buy a new shirt, she reasons, without anything being wrong with all your other ones.

Sam and Jan got me thinking. (You'll notice it took two of them.) It's not so much that the words or phrases are used frequently; much of language falls under that category. For instance, what should we say to someone when celebrating the anniversary of their first appearance on this earth? Is the whole "Happy Birthday" thing getting old?

What if that new shirt that Jan refers to doesn't fit? That makes the shirt wrong. And if the new shirt fits but is worn over and over again, it becomes a cliché. The use of some words and phrases is indeed wrong, but certainly not all of them.

I don't believe any of the following examples are clichés. That's too grand a subject for this little column. But some of them are overused, some are overused and wrong, and some are just flat wrong.

For instance:

Prioritize. Putting *-ize* on the end of a noun or adjective to make a verb is almost always deadly. We have come to accept many -ize words, such as alphabetize and pasteurize. But there are borderline acceptable examples like legitimize and colorize. Then there's the realm of the transcendently bad. One of my instructors in art school came up with one that made my ears hurt. When he was asked about plans for the coming semester, he said they weren't concretized.

If you use a word or phrase, you should be able to tell someone what it means. You should know that *synergy* means combined or cooperative action or force, especially in the human body, and that a *paradigm* is a model or pattern.

Touch base in the sense of "communicate briefly" doesn't really make sense to me, but then neither do many sports. On the other hand, *face time* is both innovative and titillating, implying that the encounter might evolve into something beyond a business meeting. Provided of course that your counterpart is a representative of your preferred gender.

Picking your brain sounds gross.

Moving/ going forward is verbal filler maybe a half a step above *You know what I'm saying?*

I never heard a good reason for changing personnel to *human resources* unless it's because people had trouble spelling the former.

Failure is not an option. Neither is pretentiousness.

I loathe *thank you in advance* because in my experience it usually comes from a person above you in the hierarchy and they're emphasizing the fact that you have no choice but to comply.

And here are some current nuggets that didn't find a home in my pseudo-memo:

At the end of the day means *when all is said and done.* Both are acceptable, with the former ringing more poetic to these ears.

The wrong place at the wrong time. Whether this is correct or incorrect depends on what is being described. I hear on-air news reporters say this all the time when referring to, say, the victim of a drive-by shooting or some other crime where they turn out to be an unintended casualty. That poor soul was not in the wrong place and it was not the wrong time. They had every right to be there then. "Wrong" should be applied to the perpetrator, not the victim.

What went down. This is the same reporter trying to be cool and hip, but instead coming off as tragically un. Just say "what happened."

Ironically vs. coincidentally. Many people confuse the two. Coincidence is two things happening at the same time, sometimes implying a causal relationship. Irony adds an absurd, seemingly illogical, twist. Two brothers in separate cities each getting hit by a bus on the same day is coincidental. Both of these brothers being advocates for pedestrian safety is ironic.

Taken back, as in shocked and amazed, is wrong. The correct term is *taken aback.* (It's actually a nautical term, as is *by and large.* Look them up.)

If you have favorite no-nonsense words and phrases and expressions, keep using them. Just be sure you know what they mean and that you intend them to mean something.

Thank you in retrospect for reading.

27

The Hills Are Alive With the Sound of Umbrage

IF A WORD SOUNDS WRONG, PICK ANOTHER ONE

Just when you catch yourself thinking that humankind has turned the corner and become smarter, someone snaps you back to reality by acting as dumb as a box of raisins.

I'm paraphrasing a news account from one of our more imposing metropolitan areas which quoted the city's mayor as saying that he will rehire a former aide who had recently resigned because some municipal employees were offended that the aide used the word 'niggardly' in describing how he would have to manage a tight budget.

We have three raisin-heads here, the mayor, the aide, and the staff member who took offense. The mayor, who is African-American, should not have accepted/ demanded the aide's resignation for using a perfectly good word. The aide, who is

Caucasian-American, should not have used the word in front of the two staff members, one of whom is African-American. And the offended staff member should have listened to reason.

"Niggardly" means sparing, stingy. It's been traced to the Middle English word *nyggard* in the 1300s. It means "miser." The word has no etymological relation whatsoever to the "N" word, but that's not the point. The point is that the size of the aide's vocabulary is in inverse proportion to his sensitivity to language.

Would I tell my Chinese friends I have a chink in my armor? No. Would my Jewish friends object if I got the heebie-jeebies? They should. Would I suggest that a Puerto Rican cleaning crew use Spic 'n Span? I would be loco.

The word *chink* means crack, cleft, or fissure. It's from the Middle English *chine*, meaning the same thing, and has nothing to do with China. *Heebie-jeebies* was invented in the 1920s by cartoonist Billy De Beck for his *Barney Google* comic strip and has no ethnic connotation. Michael Quinion of the web site World Wide Words says *spick* means neat and clean, and *span* means new, coming from the old expression "spanne new."

Obviously, you can't explain the derivation of every expression you use in a conversation (unless you want to extricate yourself from that exchange in a big hurry). Whether you're speaking, writing, or just having a conversation, you need to have a sense of what your listener or audience will understand or relate to.

The aide's goal, presumably, was to impart meaning, *i.e.* the fact that budget concerns meant that spending cuts were necessary. But the intended meaning was obliterated in the mind of the staff member as soon as s/he heard the offending word. The focus was suddenly on the offense and not the intent. The failure here was mainly on the side of the aide. The Oxford English Dictionary catalogues half a million words, several of which mean "stingy." It would have been a simple matter to pick one of the alternatives.

Having said that, the staff member must own up to some raisinosity in this mess. S/he probably received an explanation from the aide as to the true meaning of the word, but s/he wasn't having any. Too much umbrage to take here; can't be bothered to understand what my co-worker really intended. The staff member only knew what the word sounded like, not what it meant or where it came from. And to turn down free knowledge is dumb.

Don't call me on my use of "dumb." I know that the traditional meaning of the word is "mute," but I'm speaking colloquially. What's more, I draw a distinction between dumb and stupid. Dumb is momentary and a matter of choice. Stupid is permanent and something you're born into. And no one involved in this affair is stupid. After all, the mayor rehired the aide.

A later news account quoted the aide as saying that, in the future, he would use the word parsimonious instead. Unless he was joking, this statement shows that he still needs to raise his sensitivity a notch or two. A listener who doesn't know the meaning of niggardly stands a good chance of having a problem with parsimonious, too.

Even all these years later, political correctness is still alive and well. I await a strong letter from the raisin lobby.

28

Appeasing Aunt Ethel

COMMUNICATION THROUGH CELEBRATION

To borrow the first few lines from Spencer Tracy in *Father of the Bride*: "I would like to say a few words about weddings. I've just been through one. Not mine; my daughter's."

Made nearly 60 years ago, the movie still resonates on a sentimental level. Most people will watch it and weep at the characters' individual realizations of the changing roles they play in each other's lives. Others will mist up at the prices of the day. 20 cents a gallon for gas, 75 cents for a pound of sirloin. But they react without considering contemporary dollar value.

The father in the story, Stanley Banks (Tracy), goggles in disbelief at the $400 price tag on the wedding cake. When you consider that the mean annual income in 1950 was around $3,000, Stanley had every right to be aghast because that cake would have cost the average Joe Lunchbucket around six week's salary. In 2007, Emma's bouquet cost more than Stanley's cake. And there were people attending this wedding who were old enough to remember 1950's prices.

But a wedding is not about cost. (Not entirely, anyway.) The nuptial gala was a blend of traditional and non. The gown was champaign and pale gold. The tuxedos were black. But the cake was a spectacular Devil's Tower of a testament to sugar and flour. Strawberry sauce ran in frozen rivulets down terraces of dark brown icing, embracing boulders of ripe strawberries. Emma and Tony wanted black icing, but dark brown was as close as the confectioners could get.

A wedding is an exercise in communication, sometimes subtle, sometimes in-your-face. You're communicating to the one you're marrying, of course, in the form of "I do." You're also communicating who you are to the assembled throng by the tone of the whole production. I use the word "production" because that's what the wedding was called in the invitation.

Two things most strongly communicated at a wedding are style and attitude. In the 1950 movie, the style was traditional and expected, and the attitude respectful and prosaic. Emma and Tony expressly did not want to offend or upset anyone, but at the same time they did not want to kowtow to the lowest common denominator in fear of upsetting any pedestrian "Aunt Ethel" attitudes. (Don't fret ... neither of them has an Aunt Ethel.)

Emma and Tony communicated a unique style, evidenced by the fact that her stepfather, Pat, and I both walked her down the aisle while wearing sunglasses and carrying drinks to the melancholy strains of Judas Priest's "Hellion/ Electric

Eye." It also communicates an attitude: not "in your face," just "our way."

(The choice of music makes more sense when you realize that the majority of the wedding party comprised rock musicians.)

Traditional and non: Emma tossed the bouquet, but she did it while wearing a specially designed black T- shirt over her gown commemorating their union.

Non: Tony didn't throw the garter. He was busy putting on a rollicking show with his band, Two For Flinching, throughout the dancing part of the reception.

Some of the ideas did not get to come off as planned. Emma had originally wanted the assembled guests to hold lighted sparklers as Pat and I walked her down the aisle. But the idea was deemed a safety hazard because there was way too much polyester in attendance and no one wanted an accidental fabric test. We safely lit the sparklers later, unbeknownst to the owner of the reception hall.

The color scheme was red and black. Black tablecloths with red napkins, black tuxes with red bridesmaids' dresses. It's not a tribute to the French writer Stendhal, Emma just happens to like those colors, and Tony wears black as a matter of course.

Style is relative. I threw an engagement party for them here in Pittsburgh for friends and family who weren't making the trip to New York. If I communicated anything, it was informality. We sat and told stories, munching on such delicacies as a tasty deli ring sandwich and macaroni salad and throwing back cold Molsons and popular soft drinks. No suits or gowns, just jeans and nice summer clothes.

Someone should have done a little communicating with the Jamestown Chamber of Commerce because the weekend of the wedding coincided with the annual Lucille Ball Festival. The late actress was actually born in Celoron, an aneurysm in the road just west of Jamestown, but Jamestown appropriated Lucy as its claim to fame. A friend told me that when he tried to make reservations, all the hotels told him they were full. He later found out that that's what they told you if you were staying only one night. I was staying for two, so I had no problem finding lodgings.

I met the lead singer of Tony's band on the evening of the rehearsal. Her name is Teal, and upon seeing me for the first time, she exclaimed how nice looking I was. It was flattering that an attractive woman thought I was as cute as a flying squirrel even though she's young enough that her mother could have been born the year I graduated from high school. Apparently, she was dazzled by my patented T-shirt-blazer-and-jeans ensemble. Again, style and attitude will tell.

Emma and Tony communicated just between themselves, too, in the form of an in-joke that they meant to explain but never got around to. Each place setting at the reception featured a favor in the form of a small sealed black paper bag. Inside were a bunch of red and black M&Ms and three sugar packets. The candy was a no-brainer, but the packets posed a puzzle.

In the two years they've known each other, Emma and Tony have eaten in a lot of restaurants. A *lot* of restaurants. They fell into the habit of always taking four sugar packets away with them. They had accumulated drawers full of sugar packets, so they figured this was a fine way to dispose of them. I'm actually glad they didn't explain the sugar. Perplexed people are fun to watch.

The only sad note was played after the wedding. A skilled stone mason and owner of his own company, Tony's dad was at once pleasant and rough-hewn. The highest tribute I can pay him is that he was a nice guy. Tony, Sr., was seriously ill at the time of the wedding, but he got through it well and had a fine time. He achieved his goal: he lived to see his son get married. He died 10 days later.

In this little production, if I may say so myself, the fathers of the bride were class acts. And so, especially, was the father of the groom.

29

The Code of the West

AND THE EAST ... AND THE NORTH AND SOUTH

During the media melee that was the O.J. Simpson trial -- (I refer to the murder trial; the sports memorabilia version is no doubt on the way) -- a witness described the voice of an unseen person near the crime scene as having "sounded Black." Simpson's attorney, the buoyant Johnnie Cochran, sprang to his feet and objected, sputtering, "Sounded Black!? That-that-that's racist!"

I've always believed that the reason for the hesitation in Cochran's bluster was that even he didn't believe it. Because on an earlier occasion, after a botched take for a Hertz Rent-A-Car TV commercial, Simpson himself is reported to have said, "Damn, I forgot to talk White."

It's still not politically correct to say this, but it's fundamentally obvious that different accents and dialects exist as a result of cultural and linguistic variety. (I use those adjectives because race and ethnicity have nothing to do with it.) Adopting an accent or way of speaking that is different from your baseline accent or manner is what linguists call code shifting. Well-spoken politicians and well-trained actors can turn it on and off at will. The rest of us can do it to varying levels of success, sometimes consciously, often unconsciously.

I was in Atlanta, Georgia, several years ago for a series of meetings. I hadn't been there an hour before I found myself adopting the slow, leisurely pattern of speech that prevails there. In Atlanta, it's less about accent than pacing. They're just in no hurry to finish a sentence. My code shifting started unconsciously, but then I realized I was doing it. Linguists believe that the mimicry comes from a desire for symmetry, a desire to fit in.

(Ironically, the only word they're in a hurry to say in Atlanta is Coca-Cola; many natives pronounce it "Co-cola." Doubly ironic because guess where the company makes its corporate headquarters.)

Sometimes the code shifting comes from an emotional issue. I dated a woman once years ago who spoke with a charming Irish accent as her baseline. But there was one time she was extremely upset at something I did, and she started speaking in a generalized Southern accent. And she wasn't even from the South. (That bears further research.) And no, I won't tell you what I did that irked her.

Understand that adopting the accent is usually a matter of choice and preference. While it bothered me not at all to slide in to the Atlanta accent, I draw the line at Pittsburghese.

Here in southwestern Pennsylvania, we're famous for saying 'dahntahn' for 'downtown' and 'yinz' for the second person plural pronoun 'you.' This accent grates on the ears of most outsiders on a par with the New Jersey and Brooklyn varieties.

Good communicators adopt the language patterns of their listeners, not just so they'll be understood, but so they'll fit in. But code shifting happens physically as well as linguistically.

"Match and Mirror" is a term used in the study of body language to denote shared posture. If two people are having a pleasant and an involved conversation, they will often adopt the same posture unconsciously. In its pure, unmanipulated form, this physical code shifting shows two people in total balance, symmetry, and agreement.

I once saw a young man and woman meet for the first time in a café. The first good sign was the chairs they chose at the small, square table. They sat at right angles to each other, which is much friendlier than the adversarial seat directly across the table. As they chatted over their coffees, I saw that they were both sitting in the same position: one forearm on the table and the other holding the cup.

At one point, the woman lifted her hand to scratch her cheek. The man's hand shot up to his face. He wasn't purposely matching her, he was just completely smitten. It was heartwarming to watch.

You'll often see two people in conversation demonstrating not only the principles of match and mirror, but the listener will nod his/her head in time to the rhythm of the speaker's words. If your listener does that along with matching your posture, you can be sure they agree with you. If it's unforced, that is.

Like anything else good and pure, code shifting and match and mirror can be corrupted. Many people in sales are trained to watch for positive and negative nonverbal signals from their prospects, and to match their counterpart's positive posture and moves when appropriate. But this is deadly dangerous and must be done discretely because there's a good chance the person being matched will notice the matching.

Even in simple, one-on-one conversations outside of the sales arena, you can often use the principle to put your conversational partner at ease. By adopting their posture, you're putting yourself in sync with them and helping them to relax and converse more comfortably. Let common sense prevail, however. If they're demonstrating anxiety or defensiveness, it doesn't make sense for you to match those moves.

Don't call attention to or talk about these principles of code shifting in language and posture if you want the conversation to flow naturally. When I give my *You Don't Say!* seminar on nonverbal communication, people in the audience become self-conscious and are afraid to move, unless I point this out and allow them to relax. The same thing will happen to you; your partner will suddenly shift focus from the topic to themselves.

And all the objections in the world won't get them back on track.

30

Eye Direction and Lie Detection

THE EYES DON'T HAVE IT. WELL... NOT ALL OF IT

Many myths exist about nonverbal communication, and one of those myths is that an indicator always means the same thing. Crossed arms always mean defensiveness or disagreement. Not always; sometimes you're just cold. Speaking in a louder or higher pitched voice is always a signal of lying. Not always; sometimes you're just nervous. Standing too close to someone during a conversation always means you're aggressive. Not always; sometimes you're just cold.

Much has been made of the fact that our eyes move in particular directions when we think of particular kinds of things. I once saw an episode of *CSI: Crime Scene Investigation* in which one of the investigators decided that a suspect was lying because her eyes darted to one side when she answered a crucial question. While that plot point was based on fact, it isn't that easy, no matter what television scriptwriters and some body language books say.

We've all heard that shifty-eyed people are liars, or at the very least, untrustworthy. Actually, eye movement is a sign of mental activity. The lights are on *and* somebody's home. But what kind of activity? In his book on neuro-linguistic programming, *Modeling With NLP*, Robert Dilts says that when the responder to a question looks to the left when answering, he's remembering, and when he looks to the right, he's constructing. (Dilts isn't the only author who says this, but I liked his little eye diagram the best.)

The question-asker needs to pay attention at these times, because some of these eye movements are fleeting. But if she pays too much attention, the questionee might sense that she's up to something.

Dilts and others also note that if one is thinking of something visual, in addition to his eyes moving either left or right, he will always look up. If the thought is aural, the eyes will move directly to the side (toward the ear). If it's a feeling or emotion, they'll look down. But Dilts makes no distinction relating to handedness.

Some experts would agree with Dilts's diagram of left and right eye directions, but only for right-handers. With left-handers, they say, the directions would be opposite, so you'd need to adjust the concept for eight to ten per cent of the population. This makes things very confusing.

Even more confusing is the fact that not every "expert" draws the distinction regarding whether the subject is left- or right-handed. What's an eye-reader to do? One expert seems to have solved the problem.

In *Conquering Deception*, Jef Nance says to establish a baseline norm for eye direction, then look for discrepancies. Jef-with-one-*f* has the street cred for this sort of thing as he's a certified fraud examiner and a former undercover narcotics agent. In these roles, he's interrogated his share of evildoers.

First Nance asks the subject a question that would obviously call for remembering and about which he would have no reason to lie, like his mother's birthday, his license plate number, the last time he ate pizza, and the like. Let's say the subject is right-handed and his eyes move to the left when answering these questions.

Then Nance asks a question that would call for constructing an answer. For instance: What would your dad do if your mom forgot his birthday? How would your aunt react if your mom served her sushi? His eyes should move to the right, and for the sake of argument, let's say they do.

Then after the norms for remembering and constructing have been established, Nance asks the important questions. Where were you on the night of October 30? And if the subject indicates that he's "constructing" an answer to a question that should call for "remembering," he's not being forthright.

Please remember that constructing does not automatically mean lying. When a person uses his brain to construct an answer, all it means is that he's putting together elements or concepts that he's never put together before. In some cases this is called lying; in other cases, it's called imagining or fiction writing or calling in sick. But if the question is one of the simple remembering variety, there shouldn't be any constructing going on.

At the beginning of the column, I mentioned that many signals in body language are inconsistent, and that includes eye direction. Beyond the factor of handedness, where the meanings of the eye directions might be reversed, some people are so dominantly right- or left-brained that their eyes will go consistently one direction no matter whether they're remembering or constructing.

Remember:
*The left brain is the practical, logical, language side.
*The right brain is the impetuous, emotional, artistic side.

Obviously this process is far from foolproof, but it has obvious benefits for participants in a job interview or for parents who want to find out what their kids are up to. It can take a while for serious interrogations, but it doesn't have to for the casual interview or conversation.

The real question becomes, do you want to pay attention to eye direction or just have a nice chat?

Look me in the eye when you answer, but don't stand too close.

31

Cultural Turns

WALK A MILE IN SOMEONE ELSE'S ZORIS

Culture is our surroundings, our environment, all the spoken and unspoken social influences that make us act the way we do. We are not born with a particular culture, we're born into it. There is nothing genetic or hereditary about it; culture is always learned. But the most fascinating aspect of cultural studies is the fact that there are two kinds of culture.

The most obvious kind is visible culture, often called manifest culture. It's the rules and regulations, all the official instructions that we can refer to if we need to know how to handle a situation. OSHA regulations: hard hats will be worn at all times. Rules of conduct at the playground: no running by the pool. Traffic laws: right turn on red.

All 50 states and most of Canada allow the RTOR. You come to an intersection where the light is red, and if you want to turn right, you can ... as long as you come to a complete stop, no traffic is coming, and you don't run over any pedestrians. That's official. It's in the driver's manual. Look it up.

That's easy. The tricky part is when you get to invisible culture, or tacit acquired culture. Nobody writes these rules down, unless it's in one of the self-help books for travelers navigating a new culture. But you don't see any books for navigating subcultures in your own country. You're on your own.

I use a Pittsburgh-based example in my Cultural Dynamics program. Here in our western Pennsylvania city, we have a quaint tradition called the Pittsburgh Left. Imagine: you're at a red light, and you want to make a left turn onto a two-way street. Traffic is waiting opposite you to move straight through the intersection. When the light turns green, instead of yielding to oncoming traffic before making your left, you cut in front of them. That's invisible culture and you've just broken the law. But are you breaking a rule of invisible culture if you cut people off? No. In fact, you're breaking the rule if you don't.

I've witnessed the Pittsburgh driver waiting to go straight actually wait for the left turner to cut him off. The infraction is expected. I'm one of the few who do not make the Pittsburgh Left, and the drivers opposite me are invariably surprised.

Can you change cultures? Yes, but don't take the Pittsburgh Left to other towns; it doesn't travel well. When traveling, you need to learn the new culture, and sometimes it isn't easy to overcome the old programming.

I taught college-age students for 25 years. One day I indicated to the class that everything was okay, and a student got upset. My indicator was the "OK" sign, the circle made with the thumb and forefinger. When I made the gesture, a young lady jerked in reaction.

She was from Venezuela, and that's an obscene gesture there, in other Latin American countries, and parts of Germany and Russia. Now understand that she had been in the United States long enough to know intellectually what the gesture means here. But that intellectual knowledge was swimming upstream against a lifetime of programming that says that gesture is a bad one. She was aware and making an effort to adapt. Not everyone does.

Actor Richard Gere recently caused a lot of folks in India to pop their chutney when he put his ballroom dancing moves on an attractive Bollywood actress. He was onstage with Shilpa Shetty at an AIDS awareness rally in New Delhi, and he was so smitten with her that he was nuzzling and hugging and kissing her on both cheeks. This happened in front of an audience of Indian truckers who were cheering them on. The actress was laughing, but uncomfortably, probably because she knew what was coming.

Gere's actions cause a riot in Mumbai (Bombay) because the Hindu religion and Indian cultural norms forbid public displays of affection. They were burning the actor in effigy and calling for the death of poor Shilpa Shetty. He's a world traveler and should have known better. She was a victim, trying gamely to make the best of a bad situation caused by a foreigner who hadn't read the rule book.

Both visible and invisible cultures can be navigated as long as you're alert for cultural traps. Left turns in front of oncoming traffic work in Pittsburgh; but that's invisible culture, and I make no guarantees as to what might happen elsewhere. No one was wrong when I made the OK sign and the Venezuelan student got rattled. It was an example of invisible cultures not matching. Richard Gere was wrong when he put his dancing moves on the Indian actress. He violated visible culture; those rules are written down. Some gaffes are easily forgivable; others take more effort.

32

Writing Avoidance: The Duck Dodge

AVOID THE EXCUSES FOR NOT WRITING

I walk three miles a day, trekking up and down the hills of my neighborhood. The streets are a mixed blessing for walkers: there isn't much traffic, but there aren't many sidewalks either. The thing I like most about the suburb of Pittsburgh I live in is that it's teeming with fauna: deer, raccoons, squirrels, chipmunks, and birds of many species, including the larger fowl, turkeys and ducks. They say that turkeys aren't the sharpest tools in the shed. Maybe, but at least they get out of your way. Not the ducks.

Early one Saturday morning, I came walking around a bend and saw a mother duck leading a procession of seven ducklings across the street. The last little one had just started to waddle across the roadway when the next to last one in the queue decided to plop down and take a rest in the middle of a traffic lane. Immediately, all the other young ones did the same thing. Mom just stopped and stood there, three quarters of the way across the road, her brood strung out behind her. Of course, at that moment a car came from the opposite direction. The driver had to stop because Mom and the kids weren't moving, not even with a ton of vehicle looming over them, and because the street is so narrow that the driver had no hope of maneuvering around them.

If you're thinking this is some perverse, *Mutual of Omaha's Wild Kingdom* lead-in to an article about writing, you're right. Maybe you remember that show, with aging naturalist Marlin Perkins and his young assistant, Jim Fowler. Marlin always narrated their adventures, and he seldom got involved in anything dicey.

At some point in every episode, we would hear something like this: "While Jim wrestles the giant grizzly bear, I'll inventory the tent stakes." The other signature narrative device was the blatant lead-ins to the commercials: "Just as the mother grizzly protects her cubs from danger, Mutual of Omaha protects your family from the dangers of – " You get the idea. And their names were perfect. After all, you'd expect a Jim Fowler to be tussling with wild creatures, just as you'd expect a Marlin Perkins to sell you insurance.

One duckling got tired, and he stopped in a bad place. In fact it was dangerous, in an actual *Wild Kingdom* way. The results of not writing are not physically fatal, but they are hazardous to creative momentum. Sure, you'll get tired of writing; we all do. But if you stop writing for too long, you might not start again. You might get distracted by counting tent stakes, which is much easier (and with a more guaranteed result) than wrestling that grizzly called writing. You're drawn to the mundane task because you know you'll succeed in counting all the stakes and have a complete inventory. There's no guarantee you'll beat the bear.

Maybe you've heard some of the so-called rules for writing. One that I see often in various self-help books for writers says that you should write every day. Even if you have nothing in particular to say, you should sit down and put pen to paper or fingers to keyboard and hope something happens.

Duck doody.

Do write regularly if you can, but if you have nothing new to write about, do something else. Otherwise, to borrow a phrase from Truman Capote, you won't be writing, you'll be typing. Certainly you can stop the typing part of the writing process for a short time, but if you do, work on another part of the process. Organize notes. Gather material. Observe. Take a walk; exercise is great for energizing the brain. And take a recorder with you to make notes. You needn't always be writing, but if you call yourself a writer, you should always be somewhere in the process.

Don't worry about the ducks; they're fine. I had to chase them off the street, clapping and shooing loudly, two inches behind the last duckling in line. And even then, they moved reluctantly, Mom grumbling all the way.

Now, go for a walk. But if you plop down in the middle of the road, you'd better be writing.

(This page intentionally left blank.)

The Stories of Our Days

The How-to book on memoir writing

118 pages $16.95 + $4.00 S&H
(Pennsylvania orders add 7% sales tax)

Mail orders to:
Legacy Road Communications
PO Box 13008
Pittsburgh, PA 15243
☐ Check
☐ Money Order

Phone orders: 412-429-3432 Have credit card ready

For fax orders, fax this form to: 412-279-1807

☐ Visa
☐ Mastercard

Card number _ _ _ _ - _ _ _ _-_ _ _ _-_ _ _ _

Expiration date _ _/_ _ _ _ (ex. 09/2008)

Name as it appears on card ______________________________

Name ____

Billing Address ______________________________________

Address 2 ____

City ____

State/province _______

Zip/postal code ________________

Phone ______________________________

e-mail ____

For more information about The Stories of Our Days, visit www.legacyroad.net

(This page accidentally left blank.)

The Stories of Our Days Audio CD Set

The How-to audio book edition

2 CDs. Approx. 2 hours $23.95 + $4.00 S&H
(Pennsylvania orders add 7% sales tax)

Mail orders to:
Legacy Road Communications
PO Box 13008
Pittsburgh, PA 15243

☐ Check
☐ Money Order

Phone orders: 412-429-3432 Have credit card ready

For fax orders, fax this form to: 412-279-1807

☐ Visa
☐ Mastercard

Card number _ _ _ _ - _ _ _ _ - _ _ _ _ - _ _ _ _

Expiration date _ _/_ _ _ _ (ex. 09/2008)

Name as it appears on card ______________________________

Name ______________________________

Billing Address ______________________________

Address 2 ______________________________

City ______________________________

State/province ________

Zip/postal code ________________

Phone ______________________________

e-mail ______________________________

For more information about The Stories of Our Days Audio CD Set, visit www.legacyroad.net